THE
SILENT
STREAM

D1437521

A HISTORY of GRISDALE.

'THE LITTLE QUAKER DALE'.

BY

JOHN BANKS

ⓒ JOHN BANKS

Published in Great Britain in 1991

    by PENWORK (Leeds) LIMITED,
      36 WILTON CRESCENT,
      ALDERLEY EDGE.
      CHESHIRE.
      SK 9 7 RG.

DEDICATED to my GRAND-CHILDREN

    HELENA AMY KOHN
    FRANCES ABIGAIL KOHN
    ROSALIND MARION PARKES
    JONATHAN MATTHEW PARKES

and to all future young lovers of Grisdale.

OTHER BOOKS by JOHN BANKS include

    A PEOPLE PREPARED
    WHAT GOES UP MUST COME DOWN
    IS THERE A WORD FROM THE LORD?
    FUN BOOKS - for children
    NANCY, NANCY
    THE STORY SO FAR.

    ISBN 0 - 9502364 - 7 - 0

Printed by CALIGRAVING LIMITED, THETFORD.

F 98·26

FOREWORD and ACKNOWLEDGEMENTS

It is an act of considerable temerity, not to say rashness, that anyone not born in the dales should dare to write a book about them. There is so much that is undocumented and that cannot be known, and so much more that is locked in the minds of the dales people, which may only be provoked to the surface by the mistaken notions of an 'outsider' or 'incomer' like myself. Someone said : 'The dale is dead, let it die. All the tales have been told'. None of that is true. I have felt like a man who opens an Elizabethian spice cupboard only to find a multiplicity of small drawers inside, each one with its own flavour. I have written out of a love of the place, and in the hope that the growing number of people who are discovering it will love it too.

Where solid facts are scarce I have tried by the use of controlled imagination to build on those that do exist. John Keats said : 'I am certain of nothing but...the truth of the imagination; what the imagination seizes on as beauty must be truth'. The first six chapters, where written evidence does not exist, are an attempt to set the valley against the backdrop of the events of the time. These, I hope, will help the average reader to see the flow of history, though they may be considered by the historian as too 'conjectural'. From the medieval period documents do exist, and this is supremely true of the careful Quaker people. I have let such documents speak for themselves.

I am indebted to many who live in the dales today and whose families stretch back into Grisdale further than they imagined. Among these are Mr and Mrs John Lund of Roger Pot, Mr and Mrs Calvert of Low Scale and Mr David Bracken of the Firs, all in Garsdale. Mr Bracken's 'Wilkinson family tree' has been for me, in the Quaker period, like the golden thread which Jason held when he went in search of the Minotaur. What made me fear to tread was Mr Bracken's remark that, up to a few years ago, he was probably related to everyone between Grisdale and Sedbergh. So many toes to tread upon.

I have attempted in conversation with those who recall the more recent past to bring to mind things that would otherwise be forgotten. Among these are Mr Jack Thwaite, Mr John Dawson, Mr G. Spencer and the Rev. James Alderson, who has known the dale for 75 years.

My inspiration for writing was the discovery of a Saxon grave on the farm of a friend of mine. The few remains were mute reminders that so many others have trodden this way before us. They were 'silent', as the Grisdale stream is silent about those who have walked its banks in war and peace.

No doubt there is much more to be told, and much more that can never be recovered. Wainwright describes the valley as 'music but no noise; just stillness and peace'. It lies off the A 684 between Sedbergh and Hawes. Eastward is Wensleydale and westward the Lake District. It is a cul-de-sac no more than 3 miles long on the watershed of the Pennines. Visitors come into the valley on summer days by car but leave before dark. Those who know it well stay as long as they can.

I have been asked which spelling of the valley name is correct: Grisdale or Grisedale? In a far from comprehensive reading of the documents I have found 'Grisdale' in a will of 1625 and 'Grisedale' in the Brigflatts Monthly meeting minute book for 1679. Whichever spelling is chosen for the valley name the 'i' is long. I have also found Grystdayll (1530), Grisdall (1587), Grisdayll (1614), Grysdale (1623), Grisdaill (1631), Grysedale (1711), and Grysdale (1730). The 'non too literate' scribes who wrote down the wills of the dales folk spelled as they heard without any standard to limit them. The result is a mish mash of wonderful phonetic words which constantly present us with delightful surprises. I have found 'quishons' (cushions), 'anewdore' (a new door), 'sharkles' (shackles) and many more. All is obvious when you read the word aloud, you hear the sound of the past. This phonetic tendency accounts for the different spellings of the names of farms. I have left them as I found them, echoing the dialect of the time.

I am grateful for permission to quote, and re-produce, to the archivists of the County Record Office in Kendal, the Public Record Office in Chancery Lane, London, to the Quaker Meeting at Brigflatts, and to the authors of books from which I have quoted. Details of this indebtedness will be found in the notes on each chapter.

CHAPTERS - ILLUSTRATIONS - MAPS

CHAPTERS in the BOOK

ILLUSTRATIONS

MAPS

THE DRAWINGS IN THE BOOK ARE BY KATHRYN E. KOHN, and the
MAPS BY ANDREW W. KOHN. Reproductions by permission of
the County and Public Record Offices.

OYSTER CATCHER

'I sought for a subject that should give
equal room and freedom for description,
incident, and impassioned reflections on
men, nature and society, yet supply in
itself a natural connection to the parts,
and unity to the whole. Such a subject I
conceived myself to have found in a stream,
traced from its source in the hills among
the yellow-red moss and conical glass-shaped
tufts of bent, to the first break or fall,
where its drops become audible, and it
begins to form a channel; thence to the
peat and turf barn, itself built of the
same dark squares as it sheltered; to
the sheepfold; to the first cultivated
plot of ground; to the lonely cottage
and its bleak garden won from the heath;
to the hamlet, the village, and the market
town.'

COLERIDGE : Biographia I.

curlew

CURLEW

IN THE BEGINNING

The silent stream has it birth in a spring which, close to
the 2100 foot contour, is on the northern facing slopes of
massive Baugh Fell. From here, for about a mile, it rushes due
north through deep cuttings until its course is turned
eastwards by Black Hill. At this point its name on the map is
Grisdale Gill and its waters are soon increased by Cartmell
Gill and Dover Gill. How and why such names were given is lost
in mystery. After a short distance, and, as if to recognise
its increase in size, the name is boosted to Grisdale Beck and
this it remains until, moving first east and then south, its
course is turned west by Garsdale Head and it pours into Clough
River at Clough Bridge. From here the silent stream becomes
successively part of the River Lune and, eventually, the sea.

Those who follow its banks may surprise a heron silently
waiting in the shallows for an unwary trout; or they may flush
mallard or barnacle geese from the rich water meadows. All day
long in spring the ear is filled with the cry of curlew and
grouse. Lapwings dive-bomb those who come too near their nests,
and oyster catchers make jagged patterns across the sky. Snipe
'drum' in the evening air and, as night falls, there may be a
barn owl quartering the fields looking for prey. Once, for four
days, an avocet visited us and only left when the leaden sky
lifted. The meadows are golden with kingcups at this time, and
those who know most discover most for the variety is endless.

As the silent stream flows on through the Grisdale valley it
passes the equally silent ruined buildings on former farms
which date back for a thousand years. Once children played
here. The highest ruin is Round Ing. The stream next flows past
East and West Scale. These buildings retain vestiges of roof
and windows but they are now as silent as the indistinguishable
Quaker burial ground behind East Scale. There, not a single
stone marks the site. Soon Shorter Gill, Crookhow Gill and
Flust Gill join the stream at Galey Hill. That name would seem
to carry a sinister echo. Could it mean 'Gallows Hill', and, if
so, why? On the other hand it could mean the settlement where
the bog myrtle is found. Not a surprising thing. On the higher
slopes of Grisdale brow are Fea Fow, High Ing and East House.
Of these East House is the only one that is still lived in.
Together they overlook Reacher in the river bottom. Somewhere
near it, on the other side of the beck, in a place called
Stubstacks, stood the Quaker meeting house until a century ago.
Built in 1706 it was subject to floods. When Methodism took
over as the predominant faith of the valley it was described as
being in a ruinous state. It was demolished and the stones used
to strengthen the river bank. A barely discernible rise in the
ground is all that remains.

As the stream passes Moor Rigg, once a farm now three cottages, it is joined by Butter Beck which pours down past Michael's House and High Laith. These were field houses, or laithes, built to store the meadow hay and house half a dozen cattle through the long winter. Beck House was one of these. Now the stream meanders through the flatter parts of the valley which, after the last ice age, must have been a lake bed to judge by the depth of the alluvial soil which covers the gravel bottom. Here it passes Aldershaw, Rowantree, Chapelhouse and Beck House and, below Bow Bridge, Mouse Syke. By this time it has been joined by Rowantree Gill. Soon the waters of Storey Gill, Long Gill, Bushy Gill and Ceasat Beck pour under Two Hole Bridge to join it. Just below Two Hole Bridge the streams have uncovered areas of limestone pavement in which plentiful crinoids and Giganticus Productus fossils are embedded. These are the fossil remains of molluscs which filled the estuary of a shallow sea, 250 million years ago, which stretched to Scotland. As these little streams join Grisdale beck they are near Low House and Blakemire. From here the stream enters a narrow defile and pours over the waterfalls that lead it to the Clough river and west to the sea. At this point the stream meets the A684 road half way between Hawes and Sedbergh. Close by the Settle to Carlisle railway crosses the Dandrymire viaduct on its way down Mallerstang. This is very close to the Pennine watershed and at some time in the distant past the stream probably went the other way, down Wensleydale, but was turned aside by the glacial dolmens which block the end of the valley.

How did all this come about?

COWSLIP

cowslip

BEFORE RECORDS WERE KEPT

During the last ice-age, which ended about 11,000 years ago, Cumbria, like the rest of northern Britain, was covered by an ice sheet. It was, perhaps, a thousand feet thick over what is now the Irish sea. In the Victoria caves at Settle, just south of Grisdale, have been found the remains of hippopotamus, hyena, elephant, byson, lynx and, overlying them, the remains of early man. All these must have used the caves in the inter-glacial periods.

As the glaciers retreated from valleys like Grisdale they left behind them lakes which were impounded by terminal dolmens. Under the ice the melt-water channels cut their way through solid rock to form the bed of Grisdale Beck, but the valley floor is made up of a thick layer of alluvial soil laid down by the melt-water of the glacier. Where the river goes out into Garsdale, near Clough House, the narrowness of the valley shows how, many years ago, it released those lake waters. In the 1960's there was a proposal to build a dam at this point and re-impound the waters of the river and re-create the lake.

At the end of the last ice-age the hills were covered by birch and juniper, by crowberry, bearberry and moorland grasses from which the peat has been formed. Few, if any, early men would have set foot in the valley because the conditions were too bleak and the game not plentiful enough.

At this time Britain was still joined to the Continent of Europe and, as the climate grew warmer, about 7000BC, pine, oak, alder, elm and lime trees began to grow in Britain. The warming of the climate melted the ice-cap, increasing the waters of the North Sea, the straits of Dover were cut through and Britain became an island. The hunters and fishermen, who had sheltered on their way in the Settle caves, gave way to new stone age farmers and sheep herders.

In the summers of the period from about 3000BC to 1500BC enterprising groups of men made stone axes out of the volcanic tuff stone found on the screes of Pike o' Stickle in the Lake District. It was with these axes that farmers cleared the lowland valleys of oak and elm. These axes were 'roughed out' on site in the Lake District and 'finished' to a high polish and sharp edge elsewhere. They were exported and exchanged all over Britain, and even to the Continent.

A hundred and fifty years ago it was one of the interests of amateur achaeologists to collect 'celts', as they were called, and in the majority of cases where they were found was not recorded. Certainly they seem to have been found in the low lying areas where the soil was good and crops would be profitable, and it is only recently that their origin in the Langdales has been identified. It is still possible to find broken rough-outs on the screes of Great Langdale but complete axes have been found in Yorkshire, Linconshire, Wessex and Wales. They have even been found in East Germany and Gdansk in Poland. They measure, on average, about a foot in length.

We may imagine enterprising groups of men, who normally lived by hunting and gathering fruit, moving up to the Langdales in the warmer summer days and there collecting and roughing out a number of axes to be chipped and rubbed smooth, and then sharpened elsewhere. These axes would be bartered, or given as marriage gifts, and in that way transferred to some places where farmers were clearing their land. In all some 700 axes have been found, but as this represents the work of a thousand years, the number is not great. At Grimes Graves in Suffolk a comparable group of men were making similar axes and tools out of flint. (1)

After these people came the 'Beaker' people who buried their dead in pottery vessels, or buried beakers with their dead, who used bronze knives and lived in circular huts ten feet in diameter with walls made of 'dry stone' three feet thick. A centre post held up the roof. Remains of their small farms are to be found in Ribblesdale to the south of Grisdale, and their circles of standing stones dot the hills of Cumbria, and the Yorkshire moors.

From 500BC the weather turned colder and wet and the limestone areas of the Pennines were occupied because of their relative dryness. A military people who loved horses and buried their dead in chariots came into the area at this time. Iron swords with elaborate sheaths, made by them, have been found in Cottardale a few miles to the east of Grisdale on the way to Hawes.

As we come closer to the end of the millenium, about 100BC, the north of England was occupied by the Brigantes whose queen was Cartimandua and whose capital was near Huddersfield. She it was whose husband, Venutius, opposed the advance of the Romans.

. . . . .

1: Nick Higham: Northern Counties to AD 1000. Longman. London.
       1986. p317.

WERE THE ROMANS HERE?

There is no proof that any Roman ever set foot in Grisdale for they have left no mark upon the landscape. On the other hand it would be surprising if those disciplined people did not thoroughly investigate every valley which lay behind the defence line of Hadrian's wall and within the road system which crossed and encircled the area. They would argue that it was just in such areas of upland scrub forest that the guerillas might hide who could attack their military transports.

Ptolemy, writing in the first century, declared that the Brigantes of north Britain had nine major towns. These have been identified at Binchester, Caterick, Aldborough, York, Ilkley, Almondbury and possibly Huddersfield. Two others have still to be found. Away from these centres small farmers occupied the higher ground living in round huts in small enclosures. They hunted, grew barley and folded sheep. Lower down the rivers the valley bottoms were filled with swamp and willow thicket. Ingleborough, which may be seen from the Grisdale valley, was one of their fortified strongholds.

Julius Caesar had crossed the Channel to Britain in 55BC and had reached the Thames but had then returned to the continental mainland. In 43AD the Emperor Claudius wanted to secure his north west frontier, and needed to gain the prestige of conquering an unknown and savage land. He turned his eyes to Ultima Thule, or Britain. The project was so unpopular with his troops that for a month they refused to embark from the continent. When eventually they did so they met stiff resistance from the Britons, but soon the Romans had reached Colchester and by the year 48 Ostorius Scapula had cut off the Brigantes of the Pennines from the Silures of Wales by securing a base at Chester.

In 51 Caractacus of the Silures sought the protection of Cartamandua of the Brigantes but the lady put him in chains and handed him over to the Romans. Venutius, her husband, divorced her and for twelve years defended Ingleborough against all comers. In 69 he constructed the vast fortification of Stanwick five miles north of Richmond which covers 850 acres and has a defensive ditch which is six miles in circumference. In 74 Petillius Cerialis attacked and took it and the defeated Brigantes retreated into such dales as ours.

Those whom the Romans captured were used as slaves in the lead mines of Grassington and Hurst. Four pigs of lead, each weighing about 200 pounds and marked with the insignia of the supervising legionaires, have been found in the Dales. Their dates are between 49 and 117. Perhaps they were stolen and hidden with the intention of eventual recovery.

Shortly after the campaign of Petillius Cerialis Agricola became governor of Britain and began to link the civilian, settled, part of the country south of the Fosse Way with military roads leading north on either side of the Pennines. These eventually supplied the troops who manned Hadrian's wall. The eastern road ran from Lincoln through Castleford, Tadcaster, York and Piercebridge to Newcastle. The western road ran from Chester through Northwich, Manchester, Ribchester, Overborough, Low Boroughbridge and Old Penrith to Carlisle. Another major road crossed the Pennines from east to west just north of Grisdale. It ran from Piercebridge through Greta Bridge, Brough and Bowes to join the road to Carlisle. A further road travelled eastward from Lancaster and can still be followed near Hawes. It eventually came to the camp at Boroughbridge.

One of the few spare time pursuits of a Roman officer serving in such a distant outpost would have been hunting. 'Are you reading, fishing and hunting or are you doing all three?' Pliny asked his friend Caninius Rufus. (1) Britain abounded in game and had larger animals such as bears, wolves, deer and wild boar in plenty. Britain was also famous for its large hunting dogs, which resembled mastiffs, and could tackle a stag or a boar. Heavy iron spear heads have been found which may have been used in such chases.

Wild boar hunting was a dangerous sport and the dogs were equipped with leather collars, studded with iron, to stop them from becoming casualties. Nor were the hunters always safe. Ausonius warned his friend not to get too close to the animals, and reminded him of the wounds his brother had suffered. On the moor above Stanhope was found an altar to Vinotonus (the same as the Roman god Silvanus, the god of hunting). It had been erected by a Roman cavalry officer, Gaius Tetius Veturius Miciamus, in gratitude that he took 'a wild boar of remarkable fineness' which no one else had been able to kill. (2)

Cicero is doubtful if such a savage sport could please a cultured mind:

> 'What pleasure can it possibly be to a man of culture, when either a puny human being is mangled by a most powerful beast, or a splendid beast is transfixed with a hunting spear? And even if all this is something to be seen, you have seen it more than once, and I, who was a spectator, saw nothing new in it'. (3)

On the other hand a cavalry officer deprived of the softer pleasures of Rome might not share his scruples, and would take what was available.

It is possible that Grisdale, which got its name hundreds of years later in the Viking age as 'the valley of the wild boar', could well have been a weekend place of retreat and sport for

Roman officers from the nearby forts of Galava and Boroughbridge. There is one other tantalising hint of such a possibility.

In France, in the late seventeenth century, was discovered a small circular bronze plate now in the Bibliotheque Nationale in Paris. It appears to be a piece presented by the officers of the twentieth legion (Valeria Vitrix) to an Aurelius Cervianus. Perhaps he was an officer who was retiring and going home. Two legionary standards flank a Roman eagle and the legions' insignia of a wild boar and a hippocamp (a legendary monster with the head and fore-quarters of a horse, and the tail of a dolphin) are beside the names of the legions. Two ranks of soldiers face each other and the legend reads : VTERE FELIX ('Make a happy use of this'). Below the centre of the plate hunting scenes are depicted, and though we may put down the lion and the peacock to poetic imagination, or to some allusion we cannot recover, there is no doubt about the hare, the stag and the hunting dogs.

We know that the twentieth legion was in Chester and Caerleon up to about the year 250. After that we are not sure where they went. Perhaps Aurelius Cervianus went home with them and settled in France. I do not suppose for one moment that he hunted in Grisdale, but how many other Roman officers could there have been who did hunt there? They might have carried back with them a similar tropny from the officer's mess. We shall never know for the record, like the stream, is for ever silent.

. . . . .

1: Pliny : Epistulae II 8
2: Collingwood and Wright : Roman Inscriptions in Britain:
    Oxford 1965 : 1041.
3: Cicero : Letters to a Friend 7 : 1

wild boar

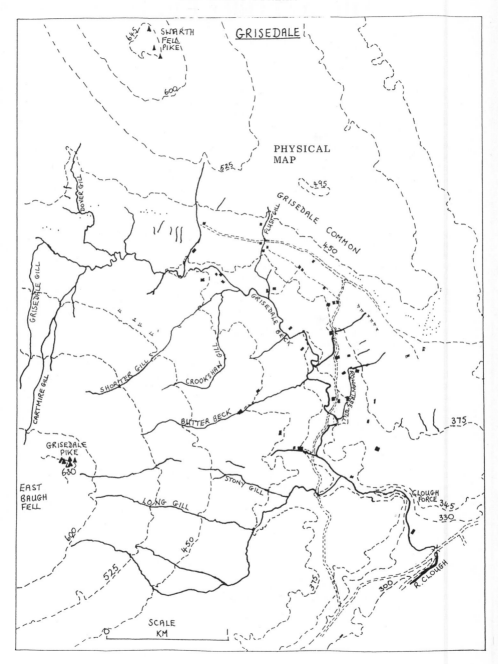

SWARTH FELL PIKE

GRISEDALE

PHYSICAL MAP

GRISEDALE COMMON

DOVER GILL

GRISEDALE GILL

CARTMIRE GILL

SHORTER GILL

CROOKSHAN GILL

GRISEDALE BECK

FLUST GILL

ROWANTREE GILL

BUTTER BECK

GRISEDALE PIKE

EAST BAUGH FELL

LONG GILL

STONY GILL

CLOUGH FORCE

R. CLOUGH

SCALE
KM

THE MATTER OF BRITAIN

In the latter years of Roman rule Britain was described as 'an opulent island'. This, at least, was true of the south and east and all that part of the country which lay below the Fosse Way. During Roman times there had been a massive increase in the population, and a money economy and the Roman peace had encouraged the growth of large agricultural estates. These villas lived by producing corn for the Roman army and by exploiting the forests and mineral resources available to them. In this way the forests were largely cleared, not only to make way for the towns and villas, but to supply the vast amounts of large timber needed to build the army's fortifications.

By the middle of the fifth century all this had changed. The prosperous villa owners, seeing which way the wind was blowing after the witdrawal of Roman forces in 410, had left. Their appeal for help to the Roman army in Gaul had fallen on deaf ears. Local self-styled 'emperors' took over and, as the forts of the Saxon shore were deserted, pagan Angles, Saxons and Jutes began to move up the river valleys of the east coast. These people had never lived in towns and were unable to take over the life-style available to them. With the decline of the towns the Christian Church, and the Bishop's sees, went out of existence, and with them the Latin language, Latin law and the customs they supported.

Though still a rich country Britain was defenceless and the barbarians took over. The uncertainty of the times accounts for the hoards of silver and other precious things wnich have from time to time been discovered. In the absence of strong rooms and banks the safest place to put your treasure was in the ground in the hope that no one would find it before you could return yourself and take it away. Some owners never returned and gold and silver hoards, like that of Mildenhall, have fallen into our hands. In the ruins of the villas excavation has shown that those who took them over, not knowing how to use their opulent rooms, built timber lean-to shelters within the walls because they did not know how to live in the places they had inherited.

In the uncertainty of the times the native Romano-British population was pushed west and, in Devon and Cornwall, many crossed over to north west France to form what came to be known as 'Brittany'. Meanwhile the cultivated land of lowland Britain returned to wilderness, waste and scrub.

Further north and west, where Grisdale lies, the people had never been softened by a Roman urban life-style for the area had remained a military zone, and those who lived in it had served the rough requirements of the Roman soldiery. The area was, at first, out of reach of the Anglo-Saxon penetration. At the battle of Mount Baden on a site unidentified, but possibly near Swindon, the Saxon advance was halted for a while. This took place about the year 500, and it was only when the Saxon advance was assumed, some forty or more years later, that the north was threatened.

It may be that the consequent resistance was tough and that small groups of north western tribesmen, riding on the sort of mountain ponies you may see on the fells above Grisdale and on the slopes of Swarth Fell, gave rise to the legends of King Arthur and his knights. The cycle of medieval Arthurian romance is a top-heavy structure raised on a very small foundation, for there is no evidence that Arthur ever existed except in folk memory or wishful thinking. Wherever the Britons defended themselves it might seem to them that Arthur could ride out of the forest to their aid.

All this might account for the traditions about Arthur which are found in the south-west and north-west. Ruined Pendragon castle in Mallerstang, the next valley to Grisdale, is his supposed birthplace. Legend has it that at Richmond castle in Swaledale the local 'idiot' boy once found a door which led him to Arthur's hall. There he saw the king asleep at the round table surrounded by his knights and a great treasure. The lad rushed out to raise the town but, being a fool, could never find the door again.

Old Barbarossa
Sleeps not alone
With his beard flowing over
The grey mossy stone.

Arthur is with him
And Charlemagne. The three
Wait for awaking
Wait to be free.

When the raven calls them
They'll rise all together
And gird their three swords on
And look at the weather.

Arthur will swear it is
A very cold morning:
Charlemagne says a red sunrise
Is the shepherd's warning.

Barbarossa says nothing
But feels in every bone
A pang of rheumatism
From sleeping on wet stone.

Then from the grey heaven
Comes a faint mist of rain
And the three sleeping heroes
Turn to sleep again.   (1)

So wrote Edward Shanks, and of such things dreams are made, but who knows how much truth there may be in them. If Arthur rode at all he could as well have ridden in Grisdale as anywhere else.

. . . . .

1: Edward Shanks, 'Old Barbarossa'.

THE SAXONS
or how all this began

Just after Christmas in 1987 my wife and I were entertained by some friends whose farm lay just over the watershed from Grisdale, and a few miles down Wensleydale, where the place names tend to end in 'by' and 'ham' and not the harder gutteral sounds of the upper dales.

I had returned from a visit to the Holy Land and as I described some recent archaelogical finds there the farmer's wife went over to the cupboard and took out of it a small cardboard box. In the box was a circular brooch about one and a half inches in diameter. It had been cast in bronze and was of a green colour. There were raised bands at intervals round the edge of it and, quite clearly in one place we could see signs of rust where a pin, which had held it into a cloak, had been before water destroyed it.

'Where did you get this?' I asked.

'We found it in a heap of stones which has always been by the farm gate. We needed some rubble for the road, so we got out the JCB and took some of the outside stones for our purpose. Soon after that a friend of ours was poking about in what was left and found this'.

The farmer's wife next produced a small plastic bag and from it laid on the table a few bones. There was the ball joint of a thigh bone, a piece of the pelvis and, to our inexpert eye, teeth of man and dog and perhaps even wild boar.

My hosts went on to say that the local museum authorities had been notified and they were hoping for a thorough, expert search. The brooch it seemed, from what they had been able to read, was identical with Anglian brooches found not many miles away.

Who was this man or woman and when did they live? What could have been their status and did their special grave mean that he, or she, was a person of some importance perhaps twelve hundred years ago? What my friend had always imagined to be a dumb heap of stones, perhaps a ruined building, could have been a grave raised over a Saxon warrior two hundred and fifty years before William the Conqueror came to Britain. William's agents had surveyed the valley in which the bones were found and recorded it in the Doomsday book of 1086, describing it as:

'In CROCSBI three carucutes taxable, one plough possible. Bjornulf had a manor there. Now the same man has [it] from the Count. The whole, two leagues long and half wide.

There are moors there. Its value [before 1066] five shillings'

They added 'It is waste'. They had seen no more than we had.

Bjornulf was obviously a Viking name, but our unknown Angle must have preceeded him by at least 250, or even 500, years; though the fact that he, or she, was buried, rather than cremated, would argue for the possibility that the burial was in the later period of Anglo-Saxon occupation of England after the population had become Christian.

What was wanted now was an expert search and a carbon dating test to unlock more of the story from that silent heap of stones.

As I returned that night to Grisdale I asked myself if the Saxons had penetrated the extra thirty miles west to include Grisdale in their sphere of influence? Certainly the place name evidence for it was lacking, though the powerful kingdom of Northumbria must have reached out to include Cumbria. It is also possible that Grisdale, and many valleys north and west of it remained an area of dispute between the Saxons and the British 'kings', who carried on an independent existence between the upper and nether millstones of Saxon England and celtic Scotland.

I can claim no dramatic beginning for my story, but I am aware of the silent valley and almost silent stream of which I write. If their story could be unlocked it seemed to me that it would be as interesting to the well-tuned ear as the bird song that fills the dale in the spring. This book is an attempt to tease a story out of the stones, the silent fells and the increasing number of documents that exist in the later period.

Through it all the stream remains the link which has bound together those who from the days of early man to the twentieth century have walked its banks marvelling at the kingcups in the spring or the jewelled stars of a winter night.

Kingcup.

KINGCUP

THE MEN WHO NAMED THE DALE

The Anglo-Saxon Chronicle records that in the year 789:

> 'There came for the first time three ships of Northmen,
> and then the reeve rode to them and wished to force them
> to the King's (Beorhtric) residence, for they did not know
> what they were; and they slew him'.

A few years later, in the year 793, the comfort and
complacency of Christian England was again shattered by Viking
raiders who attacked the coast of Northumbria. This is how the
Chronicle records that event:

> 'on June 8th the ravages of heathen men miserably
> destroyed God's Church on Lindisfarne with plunder and
> slaughter'.   (1)

From that day, for 150 years, until Eric Bloodaxe was killed
in York in 954, Scandinavian raiders increasingly occupied
large tracts of land in northern and eastern England. This was
the Danelaw. In 954 England returned to the rule of English
kings but, like Cnut, they were partly of Scandinavian blood.
William the Conqueror, who overcame England in 1066, was a
descendent of the Vikings who had settled in Normandy.

From the point of view of Grisdale the Danish raids, the
payment of tribute money to buy them off over a hundred years,
and even Alfred's fight back and recovery of most of what they
had taken, are no part of the story. Eventually the Danelaw was
confined to an area bounded by the Humber to the south, the
Pennines to the west, and northwards into disputed areas of
Northumberland and southern Scotland which were fought over for
hundreds of years.

The Danes of the Danelaw have left their mark on the
landscape in many ways; but one mark of their presence is in
the many village names ending in 'by'; a Scandinavian suffix
denoting a settlement. There are 854 of these in England and
the nearest ones to Grisdale lie twenty miles over the
watershed eastwards in Wensleydale : Thoralby, Carperby,
Melmerby and Bellerby. They lie in the more fertile regions of
the country and it is thought that the majority of such names
contain also the personal name of the family who first settled
in the area.

York was the major town of the Danelaw and the excavations
recently undertaken there in Coppergate have revealed the
richness of the Danish civilization and the widespread nature
of their trade. Amber from the Baltic, silks from the eastern
Mediterranean, pottery and jewellery from Europe and spices

from the orient have been found; as well as the means to make gold jewels, do inlaid silver work and carve wood. The Vikings were not savage heathens in cow-horn helmets; they had become Christians and the merchants of York and Lincoln had commerce with places as far away as Russia.

The pressure for land, which was one of the reasons why the Viking raiders first left their homeland, had taken them also to Ireland, and Dublin became a Roman town.

The upland area of Cumbria, of which Grisdale is a part, saw little human activity for five hundred years in the second part of the first milennium after Christ. Dr Nick Higham wrote :

> 'Substantial tracts of land were under-utilised or totally unused. The prevalance of topographical names such as 'Uldale' (wolf-dale) imply that the central fells with their igneous rocks, shallow acid soils and inhospitable climatic conditions had been abandoned to the only natural competitor of man among the English fauna - the wolf'. (2)

Other place-names in Cumbria suggest that it may have been largely occupied and ruled by resident 'British' kings, or minor ealdormen from the south west of Scotland or Strathclyde. An English minster existed in 900 at Heavesham at the head of the Kent estuary and was burnt by a Viking war band in 910. Were they on their way from Dublin to found a new Scandinavian kingdom in York, or a casual war band returning home? Certainly Tilred, the Abbot of Heavesham, fled east, perhaps away from the direction from which they had come.

It appears that in the following years Scandinavian settlers moved into the upland areas of Cumbria and north Yorkshire; or, at least, used them for 'transhumance', that is, as temporary summer pasture for cattle. Two house names in upper Grisdale, West and East Scale come from the Norse word SKALI meaning a hut or temporary shelter such as might have been used by shepherds in a summer season. Grisdale itself is a Scandinavian word meaning: 'a valley where young pigs are reared', and we have already seen that Uldale, the valley just over the watershed, indicated the threat that wolves could pose to the shepherd or pig-keeper's care. Grisdale is surrounded by names of Scandinavian origin such as : Knudmanning (Knut's, or Knudman's settlement); Mallerstang (the boundry mark by a bare hill), and the word 'beck' by which almost every stream is called is from a Old Norse word : BEKHR.

Christopher Morris wrote :

> 'In the area of the Upper Pennines in the Dent, Settle and Lune Valley area, there is considerable evidence to support the location of settlements in the Viking period. There are distinctive Scandinavian features of the dialect in this area: the place-names of the Sedbergh-Settle area

are approximately sixty per cent Scandinavian in origin; the stray archaelogical finds from the area include a huge silver brooch from Casterton and a hoard from Halton Moor with a very fine torc. In addition stone sculpture from the region has distinctive features associated with Viking styles'. (3)

If you take a short walk up the Grisdale valley you will see to the south Ingleborough mountain. On the slopes of this at Ribblehead, lie the remaining stones of a Viking house. There are the inner and outer walls, once infilled with soil to preserve warmth. Over these was reared, like an upturned boat a wooden structure which would be thatched with straw or ling. Was this a transhumance sheiling? Certainly the very few artefacts found there would suggest none of the prosperity of York. A rotary millstone quern for grinding corn and four coins, one a copper coin dated about 867, point to a subsistence culture.

In the Viking period the population of Cumbria grew apace, partly through immigration, and areas like ours, which had perhaps lain unused for 500 years, may have come into use again at least for part of the year. Who knows: some of the ruined buildings now in the valley may stand on the sites of Viking 'long-houses'.

....

1: Anglo-Saxon Chronicle : B. Thorpe.   Rolls Series 1861.
2: Nick Higham : The Northern Counties to AD1000. Longman 1986
3: Christopher Morris : Chapter on 'From Sword to Plough' in
      The Vikings in England. Anglo-Danish Viking Project 1981.

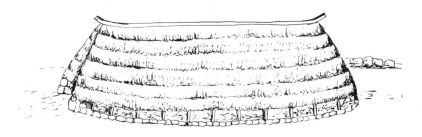

Viking Age Farm.

VIKING AGE FARM

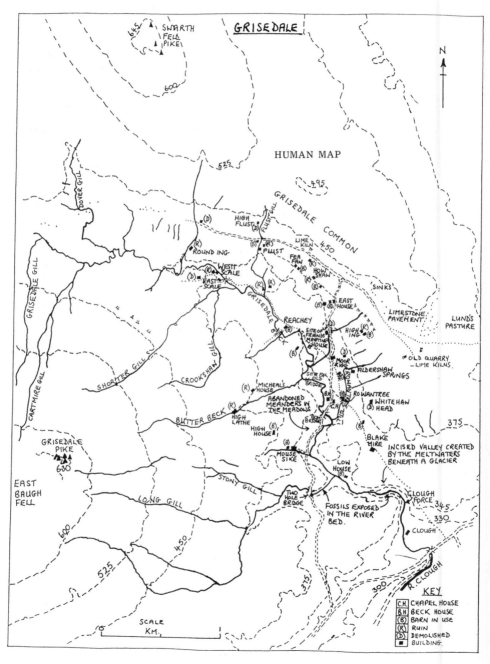

WAS IT A 'GRANGE' OF JERVAULX?

Sometime in the days of Henry III (who reigned from 1216 to 1272) the Abbot of Jervaulx was give a charter confirming the gifts the Abbey had received. Among them was :

> 'from the gift of Adam of Staveley the whole of Grisendene with all pertaining to it, to wit Ulvedale and half of Roauthaboctone and Herteron jointly, and the other half of Roauthaboctone and jointly with those of Sadberg'

Could these be Grisdale, Uldale, Rawtheybottom and Sedbergh as we know them today? Is there a difference between Grisendene and Grisdale? John Burton interpreted Grisendene as the whole area mentioned above, but including Grisdale in it. (1)

As Adam of Staveley died in 1218, and Henry did not come to the throne until 1216, we have a fairly clear date for Adam's gift which Henry was confirming as superior lord. A further charter of Henry III confirmed Alan of Richmond's gifts and added :

> 'if they find any iron and lead in their land they may mine it. And they may keep, any animals killed by wolves which they or their servants find in the forest.' (2)

The buildings of Jervaulx Abbey were begun in 1158 by Abbot, John of Kingston, and twelve monks who moved from Dale (that is Dalegrange, or Fors) where a first attempt had been made to establish a Cistercian monastery, on the gift of the founder Akarius Fitz Bardolph. At Fors they had 'erected a simple edifice for their habitation in 1145', but because of the 'poorness of the place and the intemperance of the air' they had moved, with the agreement of the founder's son, to 'a pleasant valley upon the river Eure, in East Witton, and the great pasture of Wandesleydale, given them by Conan, duke of Britanny and earl of Richmond'. They called it 'from its situation' Joreval. (ie Jervaulx) (3)

The Cistercians, an order of white monks whose original foundation was at Citeau in Burgundy in 1098, had made a conscious effort to return to what they believed was the simplicity of the monastic life which they felt had been abandoned by earlier orders. While, for example, the Benedictines accepted the gift of churches and benefices the Cistercians prefered to live in isolated places and accepted instead marginal land which they could improve by hard work. One of their ordinances read that they should live 'in places remote from the habitation of men'.

Colin Platt says :

'Cistercians rejected the proffered gifts of proprietorial churches and of manors, the working units of an economy they affected, a little self-righteously, to despise. Unencumbered lands on the margins of existing settlements were to become the basis of Cistercian agricultural economy, and it was upon these primarily that their zeal and their genius would be lavished in the creation of that characteristically Cistercian institution the monastic farm, or grange.' (4)

By the strange alchemy of history the 'other-worldliness' of the Cistercians, and their hard work, eventually made their abbeys splendid as the ruins of the wonderful abbeys of Rievaulx, Fountains and Jervaulx still demonstrate. Rievaulx was founded in 1131 and is 370 feet long and, in the minds of some, the lemon coloured stones of Fountains (founded 1132) are, in the light of a summer evening, a match for the Parthenon in beauty. Even here the original simplicity can still be seen in earlier parts of the outer walls.

'Monasticon Eboracense' lists in sixty-one closely packed folio pages the holdings of Fountains Abbey at the dissolution. There are two more pages listing the gold and silver chalices, the crosses, 'crewets', staffs and jewels in the Abbey treasury. Also listed are the 2356 cattle, the 1326 sheep, the 86 horses and the 79 swine in the Abbey's immediate holdings.

We are not surprised, therefore, that the listing for a much poorer abbey, like Jervaulx, should have extensive lands in upper Wensleydale and, among them, the marginal lands in which we are interested : 'Clough in Sedberglic, Grisendene, Grisedale, Sudeberge or Sedberge and Ulnedale'.

The only doubt that may be cast on Jervaulx's right to the whole of Grisdale is a charter of Roger of Mowbray confirming a gift by Adam of Staveley of land in Garsdale and Grisdale to St Agatha's Abbey, Easby. But the records of any manor show that small parcels of land in any area were owned by different lords, and in this way two abbeys may have been interested in our area. On the other hand it may be that the superior lordship was Easby, and the inferior lordship Jervaulx. It is also possible that others farmed parts of the valley as well, for a will of Necolas Winn of Gricedale, dated 1530, still exists. He could have farmed his land as a tenant of one of the abbeys, for the date of the will is seven years before the dissolution of the monasteries.

Also listed in Burton and Dugdale, as granges of Jervaulx, are 'free warren in Aykeberg', 'Braithwaite-grange in Witton', 'Kilgrimhou-grange', 'Melsamby', 'Newstead-grange' and 'Thirncroft' all much nearer to the abbey than Grisdale. About this sort of holding we have information which will help us to learn about Grisdale.

WAS IT A 'GRANGE' OF JERVAULX?

A grange was an outlying farm which, according to a Cistercian statute of 1152 should lie at not more than a day's journey from the main monastery buildings. Here, depending on the nature of the land, might be grown arable crops, or cattle and sheep would be fostered. The work of the grange would be carried out by peasant families, some of whom might have been given to the abbey with the land as bondsmen. Their work was overseen by lay-brothers (or conversii) who were under the control of 'the cellarer'. Such lay-brothers were in orders and observed the services of the church morning and evening but did not engage in the regime of study common to the monks. They were not taught to read and write but it is to them that we owe the beginnings of scientific sheep farming and agriculture.

Some of the lowland arable granges were large and possessed buildings which, though simple in style, covered a considerable area. The Cistercian grange of Melsonby had an inner court measuring 200 feet by 120 feet. On such a grange there would be ploughmen, carters, haywards, foresters, bakers, cheese makers, porters, swineherds and shepherds.

The size of the operation was immense. Rievaulx, at the height of its prosperity, had 140 choir monks and 500 lay brethren all of them supervising the abbey's economy. Fountains had 18,000 sheep on Malham moor alone, and many more in a 90 square mile fenced area in upper Wharfedale.

Were women to be found on the granges? We may quote an anonymous thirteenth century agricultural treatise entitled 'Hosebonderie' which said :

'it is always good to have a woman there, at much less cost than a man, to keep the small animals there and what is within the court, and answer for all the produce there as a diarywoman would',

and if we add the Gilbertine directive that 'young and pretty women should be excluded' we shall see that things have not changed much over the years.

On a large grange there would be a number of buildings including a hall, a dormitory, a barn, and buildings for cattle and sheep. There was no attempt to repeat in miniature the abbey buildings so there would be no chapel as such. In later years it became the practice for hard-worked abbots and monks to escape to a grange for a holiday away from the pressure of monastic business. There is an implied criticism in a letter from John ap Rice, one of the King's commissioners, that the abbot of Bury St Edmunds, John Reeve, was 'moche forth in his granges'. No doubt, in such circumstances, prayers and masses would be said and suitable accomodation supplied. In the thirteenth century some monks sought permission to live on the granges but such permission was only given when it was clear that their ministrations did not usurp those of the parish churches and clergy.

There is no suggestion that a grange ever existed in Grisdale. It is much more probable that Grisdale was used as a sheep range to produce the wool that was one of the great 'staples' of wealth both for England and the monasteries.

G.M. Trevelyan wrote :

'for a true picture of medieval agriculture in England we must never forget sheep farming and the shepherd's life. Our Island produced the best wool in Europe, and had for centuries supplied the Flemish and Italian looms with material with which they could not dispense for luxury production, and which they could get no where else. The woolsack, the symbolic seat of England's Chancellor, was the true wealth of the King and his subjects, rich and poor, cleric and lay, supplying them with coin over and above the food they wrung from the soil and themselves consumed. Not only the distinctively pastoral regions, the great Yorkshire Dales and the Cotswold hills and Sussex Downs and the green oozy islands of the fens, but ordinary arable farms had sheep in abundance. Not only the great sheep-farming barons, Bishops and Abbots - with their flocks counted by thousands and tens of thousands, tended by professional shepherds - but the peasants of ordinary manors themselves dealt in wool, and often together owned more sheep than were fed on the lord's desmesne'. (5)

Eileen Power mentions John Barton of Holme near Newark who put into the stained glass window of his house the words :

I thank God and ever shall
It is the sheepe hath payed for all. (6)

Sheep were kept primarily for their wool which was shipped out of York and Hull in vast quantities to Italy, France and Flanders from the monasteries where it was produced. When autumn came, because of the shortage of winter fodder, surplus sheep were slaughtered for their meat and the skins ('fells') were also exported to Europe.

It is possible that on the site of one of the present Grisdale buildings there once stood a simple monastic hut where a single lay brother, with a shepherd to help him, looked after the sheep in the valley and brought them at night into an enclosure to save them from prowling wolves. In a Jervaulx charter of Conacus, Count of Richmond, we read :

'and I order that they may possess mastiffs to keep the wolves away from the pastures'. (7)

No doubt, apart from wolves, life in Grisdale went quietly on year by year.

Colin Platt wrote :

> 'It remains possible that on the remote upland granges the community life of the lay brethren continued for some centuries undisturbed ... if there was identity between the great lowland grange and its cousin in the hills it resided merely in name'. (8)

The other possible use of any area such as Grisdale at this time would be as a 'chase' or 'forest' where game might be hunted. No doubt the Count, though he had given the land to the abbey, would still exercise such rights every now and again and visit the abbey to hunt over its lands. Burton comments under his entry for 'Wendesley' that Conan, Duke of Britanny, gave the lands north of 'Jor (Eure)...retaining nothing but the wild beasts and the custody of the forests'.

Then, as now, politics entered into a gift made by the lord for the establishment of an abbey, or for its maintenance. A lord whose lands were extensive would find it convenient to have abbeys strategically placed about them for there was a right to expect hospitality, and in a world without suitable hotels, this was a real consideration. Moreover, the Cistercians only sought marginal land and a lord might see his property improved by their hard work, and a suitable place of lodging established for himself and his retainers in an otherwise remote, and inhospitable, area.

In the charter of Henry III quoted above, in which the abbey's holdings were rehearsed, there are seven lines of summary of how the abbot had attempted to persuade Count Alan, then in Britanny, to help the abbey in the hard times it was suffering. On the whole Cistercian abbeys were not well endowed and it was two years before the Count came to Richmond and from there to his estates, and :

> 'within short time set about helping his people. He then went again to the valley to meet his barons and knights and stayed for six days without a break, nor did ever, anywhere, such a great quantity of roe deer, stags and hinds, fall to the bow and chase as then. But he was very angry with his steward, Scolland, and his constable, Roland, and others because of the number of wolves about, causing evil to men and animals. He then returned from the valley by way of the newly founded abbey where he stayed a little while eating and drinking'. (9)

The valley refered to is, no doubt, Wensleydale and, though there might be wolves anywhere on the high fells, it is tempting to think that Uldale (Valley of wolves) and the upper reaches of Grisdale, which lead to Uldale, were the areas Count

Alan was thinking about when he gave a piece of his mind to his steward and constable. It is idle to speculate on whether the abbot thought the hunting, eating and drinking of the Count adequately met his, and the abbey's, needs.

The fourteenth century was a time of trouble and particularly so for abbeys like Jervaulx which had holdings in the North Riding and on the edge of Scotland. There was a combination of economic depression, extremes of weather, pestilence and famine. It became necessary for abbots to turn their granges into 'vills' occupied by tenants for a fixed rent. Perhaps Necolas Winn was one of these. Where this had taken place it was sometimes possible, at the Dissolution of the Monasteries in 1537, for the layman farming the land to make a claim to continue to do so, and such a tenant would resist the destruction of monastic buildings which were useful to him. For this reason some have survived. In 1537 John Metcalf, who was the Jervaulx baillif at the time, was farming the Melsonby grange and was still in possession in 1543.

One of the reasons why Henry VIII was able to dissolve the abbeys so easily was that the monastic population had declined and the enthusiasm abated. Rich laymen no longer gave their wealth to an abbey as in former times, but rather to parish churches. The gifts to monasteries had been generous, and Burton quotes a Dr Inet who speculated that :

> 'Some men who made rash vows of going to the Holy Land, and had a mind to break them, were taught to commute with building of monasteries. Others, who were going thither, being uncertain of their return to their estates profusely gave them away to build monasteries' ... 'several people gave land to the religious houses with the proviso, that in case of their return from the wars, they were again to be restored to them.'

Be that as it may about a quarter of the land of England was in the possession of the religious orders by the beginning of the sixteenth century, and there were a lot of envious eyes. In the event many of the lands of the dissolved abbeys went to the younger landless members of families who were in league with the King, or with his agent, Thomas Cromwell. Attempts were made in some places to see that monastic churches became cathedrals or parish churches, and attempts were also made to see that local people obtained land, if only to compensate them for the loss of the livlihood the monastery had supplied. That is, perhaps a charitable judgement. Others say the Royal Commissioners were grasping, worldly and without a trace of spiritual feeling. Eight hundred houses were destroyed, the gold and silver was looted, the lead melted down in furnaces fuelled by the carved wood of the choir stalls. The bell metal went to make guns for the King and priceless books, deeds and manuscripts, were fed into the oven. Some opinions have it that only about a fifth of the value of the abbeys ever reached the

King. The rest was purlioned, embezzled or stolen on the way there. However, the rood screen and abbot's stall from Jervaulx are still to be seen in the parish church at Aysgarth.

Where the abbots surrendered peaceably they might be given a cathedral appointment. This was not the case with the last abbot of Jervaulx, Adam Sedbergh, who was elected in 1533. He was hanged at Tyburn in June 1537, with the abbots of Fountains, Rievaulx, Guisborough, Bridlington and Doncaster for resisting the King's depradations and taking part in the Pilgrimage of Grace. Scratched on the wall of a dungeon in the Tower of London are the words 'Adam Sedber Abbas Jorval 1537'.

So the lands were sold, or distributed, and the monastery buildings became a quarry for building stone. The gentleman's residence, built out of the abbey stone, may be visited at Fountains, as in other places.

Burton quotes a letter from Richard Bellycis who was Thomas Cromwell's agent in the dismantling of Jervaulx abbey :

'Pleasythe your lordship to be advertysed, I have taken down all the lead of Jervaulx, and made it into pecys of half fodders, which lead amounteth to the number of eighteen score and five fodders, with thirty and four fodders and a half that were there before: and the said lead cannot be conveit, nor carried until the next sobmre, for the ways of that coutre are so foul and deep, that no caryage can pass in wyntre. And as concerninge the raising and taking down the House, if it be your lordship's pleasure, I am minded to let it stand to the next spring of the year, by reason of the days are now so short, it would be double charges to do it now. And as concerning the selling of the bells, I cannot sell them above fifteen shillings the hundred; wherein I wolde gladly know your lordship's pleasure, whether I shold sell them after that price or send them up to London; and if they are sent up, surely the caryage will be costly from that place to the water. And as for Bridlington, I have done nothing there as yet, but spayreth it to March next, because the days are now so very short; and from such time as I begin, I trust shortly to despatch after such fashion, that when all is finished, I trust your lordship hath appointed me to doo; and thus the Holy Ghost ever preserve your Lordship in honour. At York, this 14th day of November 1538. By

Your lordship's most bounden beadman,

RICHARD BELLYCIS'   (10)

I think Adam Sedber would have been glad not to have been there to watch it all.

Thomas Cromwell, Henry's agent in the matter, was himself executed without trial in 1540.

. . . . .

1: John Burton. Monasticon Eboracense. York 1758 p 568.
2: Sir William Dugdale. Monasticon. London 1849 p 576.
3: Ibid p 568
4: Colin Platt. Monastic Granges of Medieval England. Macmillan 1969.
5: G.M. Trevelyan. English Social History. Longman Green and Co. London. p 7.
6: Eileen Power. Medieval People. Methuen and Co.
7: Dugdale, op cit p 572.
8: Platt, op cit
9: Dugdale, op cit p 572
10: Burton, op cit
11: Burton, op cit p 372.

wolf

GEORGE WYNNE 1584
and Winns before and after

According to a document in my possession George Winne leased Rowantree Farm in Grisdale from Philip, Lord Wharton, on the 16th of August 1584, in the 26th year of the reign of Elizabeth the First. Lord Wharton was, by this means, affirming what he could not avoid, namely that his tenants had a secure right, but he expected his chief rent to be paid at a proper time. The deeds of East House, also in Grisdale, confirm this. Mr W.T.K Garnett, who owns East House, showed them to me. They say :

> 'the residue of a term of one thousand years created by the Right Honourable Philip Lord Wharton in the twenty sixth year of the Reign of Queen Elizabeth ... by certain Indenture or Indentures of Lease unto divers persons in Grisdale aforesaid their executors, administrators and assigns together with divers other messuages, lands, tenements and hereditaments for the term of one thousand years without impeachment of waste under divers rents payable yearly to the said Philip Lord Wharton his heirs and assigns at Martinmas and Midsummer by equal portions'. (1)

That deed, side by side with my document, would suggest that in 1584 Lord Wharton was regularising his position with his tenants in the whole valley. It is possible that he acquired the dale, on the dissolution of the monasteries, from the Court of Augmentations, and was establishing his rights over it.

More than a hundred years later when George Mason made his will on November 3rd 1701 he left to his grand-daughter his house or estate at Whitewallhead with :

> 'all the Evidences and writings bellongenige the same & to her heires & Assignes for all that tearme of years in my grande lease unexpired & yet to come, and the paymt of the yearly rent of two shillings & four pence to the right honourable Philip Lord Wharton his receiver or Assignes att tne dayes & times for the same Accustomed'. (2)

According to Camden's 'Britannia' the Whartons had held the Manor of Wharton on the river Eden 'beyond the date of any records extant'. Their centre was Kirby Stephen. Sir Thomas Wharton (1495?-1568) was a tenant of Rievaulx Abbey and had held lands from them at Birkdale above Keld in Swaledale, and, no doubt, in other places. In 1522 he was engaged in border warfare with the Scots and was placed on commission for the peace of Cumberland. He became Captain of Carlisle in 1534 and Sheriff of Cumberland a year later. (3)

During the Pilgrimage of Grace in 1536 Wharton remained loyal to Henry VIII and was rewarded with the wardenship of the western marches. The Pilgrimage of Grace was not merely an attempt to oppose religious change and resist the dissolution of the monasteries; it was also a tenant's revolt against the enclosure of land and the raising of rents. The revolt had initial success in Yorkshire where York was taken by the rebels. A truce was offered, but Henry broke the terms and executions followed. In the dales area the independency of the dales' 'statesmen' was thrown into the balance and the rebels burnt Wharton's house at Kirby Stephen.

Wharton was one of the 'new' men upon whom Henry relied and his loyalty continued to be rewarded. He became M.P. for Cumberland and defended it against the Scots. With a few hundred men he met them in battle on Solway marches, where great numbers of Scots perished, and he took part in the burning of Dumfries. For these services he became Baron Wharton in 1544 and received most of the land north of the Swale from Reeth to Gunnerside when Rievaulx Abbey was dissolved. After a further rebellion of Catholics in 1569 more land came into the possession of his family and, perhaps, our dale among it. Park Hall, his house at Healaugh, still stands and he died there on August 2nd 1568.

His son, Thomas, had been born in 1520 and succeeded him. His father had been conservative in religion (if entrepreneurial in practice) but the son was steward to Princess Mary's household and was known to hear mass. When Elizabeth succeeded to the throne in 1558 he was excluded from the Privy Council and was imprisoned for a while in the Tower; but was buried eventually in Westminster Abbey in 1572.

Thomas's son, Philip the third Baron, was born in 1555 and succeeded his father at the age of seventeen. Twelve years later he granted the leases we have mentioned above including an area of Grisdale to George Winne. Philip died in 1625.

We may note in passing that the fourth Baron, also Philip, was a great dancer, a handsome man, a friend of Oliver Cromwell and a strong Puritan. It was out of the revenues of his Healaugh estates that in 1662 he arranged for the gift (still available) of over a thousand Bibles a year to children who would set to heart certain passages of scripture, and who belonged to the non-conformist churches. He welcomed Charles II in 1660 but was an opponent of the Conventicle Act by which so many Grisdale Quakers were to suffer. One of his successors, who died at the age of 33 in 1731, was president of the Hell Fire Club and lost his estates in drinking and card play. Pope called that Lord Wharton 'the scorn and wonder of our days'.

Let us return to George Winne. Unfortunately his will has not survived, so we do not know as much about him as we could wish, but he was not the first, or the last, Winn to live in

Grisdale. We do have the will of his brother, John, who died in 1596 leaving a son, Robert, and two daughters, Margaret and Elizabeth. All the wills of this period begin with the pious donation of the soul of the testator into the hand of God 'trusting (to be saved) by the death and merit of Christ's passion', but there is sufficient variation in the form of words for us to believe that we hear the true intention of the dying man. John wished his body to be buried in Garsdale Church yard and went on to mention 'a litel howse in aldershawe' and certain pieces of land named 'hayyegarth, westaldersgarth, holtstarkstead, overcakt and Calfe Flawe'. His brother, George, (with James and Robert Winn) was one of the 'four sworn on the book' to see his will performed. (4)

This Winn family was not the only branch of the family in Grisdale at the time, nor the first. 'Necolas Wyn of Grystdayll' commended his soul to 'Almyghte god and blessed lady' in 1530, seven years before the dissolution of the monasteries. He may have been a tenant of Jervaulx Abbey, as we have seen. His will is not only difficult to read, written in the script of the days of Ann Boleyn, it is also damaged. He left £6:13:4 to his daughter and asked for help for his wife and other children.

I have traced 19 wills of the Winn family who lived in the dale between 1530 and 1818. It is surprising that 9 of these wills mention no children at all, and, of the 27 children who feature in the other 10 wills, 16 were born after 1740. We do not have a complete set of wills, for names appear as witnesses for whom no wills exist, and it would be wrong to argue too strongly from silence.

Until George Fox entered the dale in 1652 there was a strong attachment to the St John's church in Garsdale, linked, as it was, to Sedbergh parish. Such an attachment was required of the people and, though they could not avoid it, their wills pay the service due. The inventory of Miles Winn [1577] was written by James Smathwhat 'clarke and minister at Garsdale'. Edmund Winn [1587] asked to be buried in his 'prish church Gravy[.] at Garsdall'. Nicholas Winn [1614] expressed the same wish, as did Isabell, wife of Bartholomew Winn, Nicholas Winn's brother. So we could go on through Leonard Winn [1631], Robert Winn [1632] to Grace Winn, wife of Robert, who died in 1651. Robert Winn had given £20 towards the expenses of a preacher in Garsdale and Robert Winn (of Sedbergh) in 1639 left his seat near the choir stalls in Sedbergh parish church to Richard Heblethwaite.

With the will of Reynold Winn [1677], which I quote in full elsewhere, such pious directions cease because he had become a Quaker. I believe he, and Anthony Mason, were th first fruits of George Fox's preaching in Grisdale. They figure large in the future Quaker story.

We know that the whole dales area, of which Grisdale was a part, was occupied by independently minded 'statesmen'. The word was used to mean a man who would not easily accept that any master had authority over him. Such men fought for the right to keep their rents fixed, and the right to sell or bequeath the land they farmed. Long before the return of Charles II [in 1660], and the victory of the High Church group in England, they were resisting the re-imposition of clerical authority from which they had been delivered at the dissolution of the monasteries. The re-imposition of Church tithes and other dues was not only an attempt to gain an income for the Church, it was also an attempt to enrich those who had taken over Church lands. The 'statesmen', some of whom had been in Cromwell's New Model Army, had gained ideas of democracy and the 'priesthood of all believers' as a result of their experiences and they were not prepared to come easily under bondage. (5)

With such ideas abroad in the community the ground had been prepared for the sowing of a variety of crops, and the 'field' George Fox looked over from Pendle Hill was more variously planted than he expected. There were Ranters, Seekers, Fifth Monarchists, Familists and Anabaptists ready to hear him and it was among such as these that the Quakers were to flourish.

As we have seen, the Winn family originally worshipped at Garsdale parish church but, if some of them had become disaffected, they could have been part of this motley collection. There is a story preserved in a pencilled note at Brigflatts meeting house that when George Fox first visited Grisdale the Rev. Richard Jackson M.A. was Vicar of Garsdale and Headmaster of Sedbergh school. It is claimed that he neglected his duties in both areas 'by giving way to drunken habits'. Certainly he was in dispute with the school governors and lost his job on March 10th 1655. The credence we can give to the story may be modified by the fact that his accuser was George Otway, brother of John Otway J.P. of Ingmire Hall. Otway was occupying the house the headmaster usually occupied and Jackson was having to live in an ale house where a dispute between the two took place. Moreover the Otway's were royalists and Richards was a Parliamentarian. Whatever the rights or wrongs of the matter an unsavoury row could have influenced an already disaffected Reynold Winn who, with others, was smarting under the re-imposition of tithes. (6)

Certainly 'Reynold Winn of Grisdale in Dent' in 1660, with certain men from Dent and the neighbouring dales, had withheld the tithes due to Trinity College, Cambridge, as 'impropriators' of the Rectors of Sedbergh parish church, of which Garsdale was a satellite. Their argument was that Dent, and Grisdale, were not part of Sedbergh, and Sedbergh tithes could not be collected from them. They cited previous attempts to collect such tithes, and pointed out that such attempts had failed. Here is the relevant quotation from the judgement given

in favour of Trinity College in Michaelmas Term 12 Charles II
[1st December 1660] :

> 'The master etc of Trinity College Cambridge, the
> impropriators of Sedbergh rectory, Edward Trott and Thomas
> Muryall their leesees, James Burton, Richard Atkinson and
> James Thompson under leeses v Reynold Wynn, John Burton,
> Thomas Middleton, Thomas Mason, Thomas Sedgwick, William
> Thistlethwaite and Edmund Dawson. Decree of the Exchequer
> in favour of the plaintiffs, that the tithes of Dent do
> belong to the rectory of Sedbergh, that the defendents
> should pay them in according to a composition dated 27th
> March 1505 between the abbot and convent of St Mary
> Coverham and 24 parishoners of Dent'.

The defendants had quoted a previous judgement which had gone
in their favour :

> 'the defendents in their answer having cited a former bill
> of the plaintiffs for tithes from 1652 to 1657 which was
> dismissed with costs in Easter term 1657'. (6)

Reynold Winn, and his colleagues, lost the action, but as
they were only made to pay at the 1505 level perhaps their
financial disadvantage was not great. It should be noted that
Mason and Dawson are names which subsequently appear, with that
of Winn, in the Grisdale and Garsdale Quaker records.

The Winn family were not, of course, the only family to live
in Grisdale but as their record begins so early, and continues
so fully, it will be illuminating to stay with them for a while
reserving other names for later chapters. It may be misleading
to speak of the Winn family. There seem to be several branches
of it at this time, and the inter-relationship is so confusing
that it has proved impossible to construct a family tree. The
bewildering custom of calling children by their parent's, and
grand-parent's, names makes it almost impossible to know which
Winn is which. There seems always to have been at least one
John Winn in the dale from 1530 to 1818, and he cannot have
been the same man; and the succession of 'Thomas's' and
'Agnes's' shows either considerable love for parents and grandparents, or lack of imagination.

In 1711 Margaret Winn, whose husband John died that year,
renounced her right to his goods in favour of her son, Thomas.
They were worth £19:2:0.

Samuel Winn of High Flust left £18:14:9 to his wife, Agnes,
in 1730. Adam Harker was a witness to the will and, in 1740,
his son-in-law, Thomas Winn, of Hawshawhead and other places in
the dale also died. Adam and Jane Harker of Low Scale,
Garsdale, appear in my chapter on the houses of the dale.

Another Thomas, of Scale, had died in 1734 and one of the two must have been the inheritor of 1711.

In 1775 a further Thomas, of Reacher, died. It is possible that Edmund Winn, who died in 1792, was his son for, as well as living at Fea Fow, he also owned Reacher and Stubstacks where the Quakers had built their meeting house in 1706.

The last available will within the period is of a further Thomas Winn of 'Stave Hall in Grisdale', a place I have not been able to identify. After this the wills of the Winn family originate from Raygill in Garsdale and further afield, though, as we shall see, there were Winns associated with the building of the Methodist Chapel in Grisdale in 1889. Perhaps these were the Raygill Winns.

A plain recital, such as this, of the names and dates of one family in the dale does not do justice to the inter-relatedness of the Quakers in Grisdale and Garsdale. The marriage register is much more revealing. In 1687 the marriage of Edmund Winn and Agnes Regnoldson took place and, within a few years, the Winns, Regnoldsons, Dawsons and Hodgsons were related. To this relationship was shortly added the Harkers, the Wilkinsons and the Close family as I shall show in the chapter on the houses of the dale. There were aunts and uncles, cousins and grandparents all over the place.

. . . . .

1: W.T.K Garnett : Indenture of February 4th 1901.
2: My main source of information on the Wharton family is the Dictionary of National Biography.
3: Lancashire Record Office: Preston. Wills from the Archdeanery of Lonsdale. Ref. WRW L. By kind permission of the County Archivist.
4: David Boulton: Early Friends in Dent. Dales Historical Monographs. Hobson's farm, Dent, 1986.
5: Papers preserved at Brigflatts Meeting House, Sedbergh.
6: Trinity College, Cambridge; Michaelmas Term 12 Chas II (1 Dec 1660) Box 17 (A2). By kind permission of the Master and Fellows of Trinity College, Cambridge.

GEORGE FOX COMES TO GRISDALE

George Fox, the founder of the Society of Friends, walked into Grisdale on at least two occasions. In 1652 he wrote in his Journal :

'I walked through Grisdale .. and some were convinced'

and later in the same year he returned to Swarthmore and :

'passed on to John Audland's and Gervase Benson's .. then to John Blakelin's and Richard Robinson's, and had a mighty meeting there, and so up towards Grisdale.'

Among those convinced were probably Reynold Winn and members of the Mason family. Fox had begun to preach in 1647 and came in 1652 to Pendle Hill where :

'from the top of this hill the Lord let me see in what places He had a great people gathered ... the Lord opened to me, and let me see a great people in white raiment by a river side, coming to the Lord; and the place that I saw them in was about Wensleydale and Sedbergh'.

He added a little later :

'I went to a meeting at Justice Benson's where I met a people who were separated from public worship. This was the place I had seen, where people came forth in white raiment. A large meeting it was and the people came forth convinced, and continue a large meeting still at Sedbergh'. (1)

By 1664 the largest percentage of Quakers in the national population was in the Sedbergh area. This arose because the Civil War, and the Puritan parliaments, had encouraged seekers for the truth to believe that 'the reign of the saints' was a possibility. During the lifetime of Cromwell Quakers were protected, but on the accession of Charles II this protection was withdrawn, despite his promise of tolerance, and his personal preference for it. The High Church party were in the ascendent and the Act of Uniformity, which imposed the Book of Common Prayer and worship in the parish churches, was enforced. Among those who would not accept enforced worship in what Fox called 'steeple-houses' were the Quakers, and their stand was attractive to the independent-minded statesmen of the dales.

In 1653 they had been described as :

'those Anti-Christians who were not free to be Tenants of other men'. (2)

Men who had been inspired teenagers in the Civil War had now grown to manhood and looked for a way to foster the expected spiritual re-generation of the nation. William Prynne quoted Jeremiah 1 v 14 against them :

'out of the north shall evil break forth upon the nation'.

Richard Baxter called them :

'young, raw professors and women, and ignorant, ungrounded people who were but novices and learners'. (3)

Despite such attacks they joined Fox in large numbers and showed their disgust with Restoration society. Samuel Pepys recorded the occasion when Solomon Eccles :

'came naked through the (Westminster) Hall, only very civilly tied about the privities to avoid scandal, and with a chafing dish of fire upon his head did pass through the Hall, crying, "Repent, Repent".

and of how, in 1664 :

'I stood by the King, arguing with a pretty Quaker woman who delivered to him a desire of hers in writing. The King showed her Sir J. Minnes, as a man the fittest for her quaking religion, saying that his beard was the stiffest thing about him. And again merrily said, looking upon the length of her paper, that if all her desires were of that length, she might lose her desires. She modestly saying nothing until he begun seriously to discourse with her, arguing the truth of his spirit against hers. She replying still with the words, "O King", and thou'd him all along'.

Pepys, like many other people, wished the Quakers would just keep quiet about their faith and so avoid trouble, for it was so easy for ill-intentioned people to blame them for national problems. He wrote in 1664 :

'all this day, soldiers going up and downe the town, there being an alarme and many Quakers and others clapped up; but I believe without any reason'. (4)

The Quakers were asking for the abolition of tithes, of the state Church and of the Universities. They also wanted law reform and religious toleration. Those who were ex-soldiers of the Commonwealth felt that this is what they had fought for then. If we add to this that Quaker meeting places were often :

'most solitary and remote from neighbours, situated in Dales and by-places'

we can see how suspicion was drawn down upon them. Because of this suspicion the Quaker Act had been passed against them in

1662 and, if a foolish action took place anywhere, they were accused of it. Being often middlemen - millers, cornfactors, merchants, grocers, bakers - it was easy in times of shortage to play on popular ignorance, and greed, and raise a looting mob against them.

In 1662 in Mallerstang, the next dale to Grisdale, Robert Atkinson, an old Parliamentary captain of horse and a former Governor of Appleby Castle, tried to lead a revolt against excise tax and chimney tax. It was timed for October 12th, but betrayed long before that. Only 30 men met at Atkinson's house and dispersed the same night. Rumour suggested that the Quakers were involved for one of the plotters, Reginald Fawcett of Ravenstonedale, had once been a Quaker. Francis Howgill, a Quaker approved minister, Robert Wharton, a shoemaker,and George Walker, a surgeon, were apprehended. At his trial Howgill said :

'Fawcett has been disowned by us these six years'

but it made no difference. Wharton and Walker were released but there was an obvious intention to make Quakers suffer. Daniel Fleming, a magistrate of Rydale Hall, had said of them :

'we have too many, this part of the country joining upon that part of Lancashire where George Fox and most of his cubs are and have been for a long time kennelled'. (5)

Howgill, Fox and Margaret Fell were sent for trial. Whatever they had done, or whatever they said and did, Quakers were trapped for they refused to swear any oath either in a court of law, or in loyalty to the King. At his trial Fox quoted, in defence of this refusal, the biblical injunction 'Ye shall not swear by anything', but as he did so in Hebrew the commonality were astonished without the justices being enlightened.

Howgill was imprisoned for life, the judgement saying 'you are put out of the king's protection and the benefit of the law', and he died in Appleby goal in January 1669. Fox was imprisoned in dreadful conditions in Lancaster but, because he still shook the country from his prison cell, he was moved to Scarborough from where he was released on September 1st 1666. Margaret Fell was not released until the summer of 1668.

These were the beginnings of Quakerism in the Grisdale area. I continue the story through the manifold local records.
. . . . .

1: George Fox : Journal for 1652. Friends Tract Soc. London. 1912.
2,3 & 5 : W.C. Braithwaite: 'The beginnings of "Quakerism' Revised 1955 H.J. Cadbury.
4: Samuel Pepys : Diary for 1662.

28 of 4th month 1754

the Books Belonging to the meeting ordered as
followeth vizt Sewils History to Thomas Winn.
1st part of Sacred History to John Wilkinson
2d part of Sacred History to Joshua Alderson
3d part of Sacred History to John Hodgson
Doctrinal Writings to George Raw
Great Case of Tythes to Thomas Alderson
John Grattons to Richard Harker
Book of Sufferings to John Raw

this Book was begun by Adam Harker then
Clerk to the meeting afterwards Robert Akerigg
was Clerk. and this Book was finished
the year 1754, by John Wilkinson.

The last page of the Men's Preparative Meeting
minute book, 1754. It lists who holds the
'library' of the meeting; and who were the
scribes.

THE MEETING IN GRISDALE

The Act of Toleration in 1689 allowed freedom of worship, and this meant that Quakers could freely build their meeting houses. Interestingly enough, Brigflatts Meeting House in Sedbergh had been built in 1675. The Friends in Grisdale had not been so bold and their meeting was established in 1690 and the meeting house was built in 1706 and conveyed in 1709.

The conveyance begins :

'A RECORD of Abstracts of the Deeds Evidences and Writings Touching and Concerning the Meeting house of the People called Quakers in Grisdale in the Parish of Sedbergh in the West Riding of the County of York

First. This Indenture Made the Eight Day of November in the Eighth Year of the Reign of our Sovereign Lady Ann Queen of Great Brittain etc Anno Dom 1709. Between Ellenor Dawson of Round Ing Widdow and her three Daughters Kathrine Akrigg Mabel Dawson and Sarah Dawson all of Grisdale in the County of York on the one Part and James Harker Michael Dawson & Thomas Winn Snr all of Grisdale aforsd & County of York aforesaid on the other part'

The house was 'lately Erected and Builded in or upon the middle of the Aforsaid Close of Ground Called Stubstacks' and the intention was that 'as much ground before the door' should be included to build 'A Porch upon a reasonable largeness'. It was also agreed that 'a stee or ladder room round about the said house for repairing of it' should be allowed and permission was given to cut a gutter to the river to carry off surplus water. All this was 'in consideration of Twenty Shillings of good & Lawfull Money of Great Brittain' which was described as 'considerable sum'. A rent of one penny a year was to be paid. A second indenture made the same day between James Harker, Michael Dawson and Thomas Winn and the rest of the men in the Quaker meeting : Edmond Winn, John Winn, Robert Akrigg, Thomas Clemat, John Close, Thomas Close, William Alderson and Thomas Winn Jnr, all of Grisdale, dedicated the house to the use of the Quaker people. (1)

The piece of land called Stubstacks, upon which the meeting house stood, is below Moor Rigg farm and by the river side. Nothing is left of it now and it needs a watchful eye to see the slight rise in the ground which is the site. The building was small and simple and was said to have held about 80 people. Being near to the river it was damp, and often flooded. No picture of it has been traced. We may ask why 'sensible' Quaker people placed the house in so unsatisfactory a position? There seems to be no answer. Perhaps the land was 'offered' to them by a Quaker family, and no other was available. Certainly it was a site central to the valley and its population.

The building of the house was clearly a co-operative venture between the Quaker families of the dale. The Dawsons were from Round Ing, one of the remotest houses of the dale, and it is possible that meetings for worship had been held in their home, and perhaps at Scale, in the days of persecution. Ellenor Dawson was the widow of Richard and was herself buried at Scale in 1709. James Harker was a member of a Quaker family which came from Swaledale : his sister, Ann, married Thomas Winn in 1689 and his brother, Adam, married Emma Wilkinson in 1703. We have already seen how the families were inter-related.

It is clear that the men and women of Grisdale, who built this meeting house, met separately each month for their Preparative Meetings for two sets of minutes have been preserved. They also met for their meetings for worship in the 'first day', and also on weeknights.

What sort of people were they who faithfully attended these preparative meetings, and were sent on the long walk to Sedbergh or Kendal for the Monthly or Quarterly meetings? While it is possible to see something of the Quaker people in general, and about the meeting house and the meetings held there in particular, it is very difficult to see clearly individual men and women who lived in the dale, and who built their houses or suffered persecution. What were the hopes and fears of these silent people who met silently in worship and were eventually buried at East Scale? Mostly we have tantalising glimpses. A name is mentioned when someone is a representative to a quarterly meeting. The names are given of two young people who want to get married, or a man is mentioned who has a distraint made against him for the non-payment of a tithe. The evidence is often very little for the meeting records are short and to the point. Most of the time we can understand the general way in which they think from what their meeting decides to do, but how the individual person thought eludes us. What went through the mind of the girl who was 'spoken to' because she had fallen in love with someone of another persuasion? What anxieties gripped the people of Grisdale, shut off as they were by the hills, as persecution came closer to them? We can only guess. Another, slightly more personal, source of information is to be found in the wills they left behind. From these we learn of family relationships, sometimes family possessions, where the family lived, and the relative wealth of the individual at the time of death, though the inventories do not include the value of the land the testators held. Bit by bit out of these silent sources I shall try to give as full a picture as I can.

The nature of a Preparative meeting is made clear by a minute of the Yearly Meeting held at Brigflatts, Sedbergh, in 1794 which said :

'This meeting agrees that the holding of preparative meetings under suitable regulations may be of real advantage where monthly meetings consist of two or more particular meetings; and that the proper business of such a meeting is, to enquire after Births, Burials and Removals, in order to carry accounts thereof to the Monthly Meetings, to read and consider the Queries as settled by the Yearly Meeting, and conclude an answer to them in writing if convenient.' (2)

The minute books of the Grisdale/Garsdale women's meeting are in a better state of preservation than those of the men and are continuous from 1709 to 1854, which the Men's meeting minutes are not. Side by side with these are Brigflatts and Kendal documents. Often one set illuminates the other. To retain the flavour of the original I have quoted them as they are, with phonetic spelling and lack of punctuation. The designation Grisdale/Garsdale is used because one set of books covered the two valleys in which the families were so inter-related.

In a bold and unscholarly hand the women's minutes begin:

'at our meeting in Grisdale the afairs of truth being under consideration we find that care of the friends is continued and nothing against but pretty well' (3)

The date of that entry was November 20th 1709 and from then on there are alternative entries for Grisdale and Garsdale, spelled 'Grasdale' on the first occasion. The same alternation is in the Men's minutes. From time to time representatives who lived in Grisdale, or from over the border in Garsdale, are sent as representatives to the monthly meeting. The building of the Grisdale meeting house had not affected the integration of the people of the two dales.

In a minute of the Quarterly meeting held at Kendal 'ye 4th of 11mo 1722' the remoteness of the area was used as a reason for special consideration :

'The Dales Friends viz Dent Garsdale & Ravenstonedale Informs this meeting of ye hardship & difficulty they Lay under in being obliged to attend ye General meetings considering how remote the(y) bye from most meets its kept at. The Stormes that frequently fall among em and the Inability to a great many to them as to Horses & wherefore desires this meeting would Indulge them in keeping their weekday meetings in ye same week ye General Meeting falls in (save wnen at Sedbergh) which for Reasons aforesaid is allowed off...' (4)

It is a matter of some astonishment to us that men and women thought so little of the great distances on foot that such attendance would entail. As we shall see, when they came to record their 'sufferings', they made journeys to York, Pontefract and Weatherby with almost as little comment.

The questions asked and answered by the women's meeting differ in emphasis from those asked at the men's meeting. Two loose, undated but early, pages give some of the questions and answers returned at one of the women's meetings. First the questions :

1 ...how power (poor) widows & women frinds (are) provided for

2 ...(h)ow frinds keep out of the customs fashions Language and habit of the world and how the Epistels from ye quarterly meeting conserning ye same are put in practice and if any frinds take liberty contrary there to whether spoken to and Exorted

3 how frinds keep first days and weekdays metings and how they keep to the hour apoynted and how frinds keep from sleping in meting and if any be not found delegent whether spoken to and Exhorted

4 how frinds that are widdows take care of ther children under their charg to keep the from companying with the worlds youth either upon account of marriage or otherwise And where any are otherwise and not carfull whether spoken to an Exhorted

5 Whether all wommen frinds keep clear in their Testimony against tythes stepelhouse layes and all things of that nature and if be not faithful whether spoken to and Exhorted

6 If frinds be carfull that no unnesseary or superfluous provision be made by women frinds at their births mariagis or burials

7 How frinds Keep out of spirit and corrupt frindships of the world and from unnessary frequenting of alehouses

8 How frinds keep their children from gooing to fairs unless their haue reall accasion

9 That there be noe tale bearers whisperers backbiters bearers of false reports among gods people but that thay speak to the party conserned first

So the document ends and it is clear that one or two questions are missing from what we see in the following written response : 'Answers to the Queris' :

1 Meetings for Worship and Decipline is kept up But not so fully attended as Could be desired, no unbecoming behaviour appears

2 Love and unity Is preserved Amongst us, to the latter part no Thing but well appears

3 Friends endevours to train up their Children both in Reading the holy Scriptures also in plainness of Speech Behavour and apparel

4 the women friends Apears clear Respecting the payment of Tithes Preist demands or those caled Church Rates

5 Friends are Carefull to avoid all vain Sports Places of Diversions And Gaming

6 Friends are just in their dealings and puntuel in fulfilling Their ingagements

7 It is Friends Care to advice If any appear inclinable to marry Contrary to the Rules of our Society

8 Wee Have no friends in our meeting that Stans need of rlief at present

9 Wee have tow friends appointed in our meeting to have the Oversight thereof and care is taken When Anything appears Amiss that the Rules of our Discipline be put in Practis

10 Friends are careful to Avoid the unneeceary frequenting Fairs

11 Wee have had no visite throgh our meeting of late

12 Wee Hope there are Soum Amongst us Endeavours through Devine asistance to Keep Clear of the corrupt Friendship And Spirit of the World, wee desire the number may be Increased   (5)

There was obviously a constant care for the poor 'that there be no beggars in Israel', and a care for the young members of the society is a recurring theme. Another recurring theme is the refusal to pay tithes. In the minutes of 1762 six women put their signatures to declarations against tithes in the following, or similar, words :

'This testimony I haue to giue Concerning tyths, I never payed nor consented to the payement of aney & I hope to bear my testimony against it whilest I Remaine hear in this world

margaret Close'   (6)

In much the same words Katharine Ayerigg, Agnas Clemey, Mabel Close, Jane Dawson and Jannet Wilkinson made their testimony. One result of reading page after cramped page of the womens' minute book is to recover the names of those who led the society. Spelling was not standard and the irregularities apply to the spelling of names. We read of :

Elizabeth Winn	Ruth Winn	Ann Wilson
Mary Alderson	Mary Winn	Ann Raw
Agnes Winn	Sarah Winn	Janet Wilkinson
Catrain Akrige	Mabel Dawson	Emma Tomson
Ann Dent	Jane Dason	Margaret Dason (Dawson)
Marey Clemme	Emma Harker	Mary Close (Cloce, Cloc)

All these date from the first 20 years of the life of the society. They can also be found in later years, and the names are still common in the area to this day. These were all from time to time representatives to the monthly meeting. Just occasionally they could not get to the town in which the meeting was held, as late in the year 1720, a note records the weather as 'stormy'.

Also recorded are arrangements for marriages between Friends, such as 'April 23rd 1713 Mikall Haygarth and Mary Clemme', or 'January 26th 1714/15 Richard Wilkinson and Janet Sutton'. . The valley must have been abounding with young life and hope. Janet Sutton became a Quaker travelling minister and liberty was given to her to visit other meetings. Among loose papers from Brigflatts is a testimony to Sarah Raw 'a minister for forty years'. It was usual for letters of commendation to be sent with such a travelling minister and the letter would be signed by everyone in the commending meeting. Here, for example, is such a letter to the quarterly meeting at Durham :

Dear Friends,

John Laycock the bearer hereof having laid before us a concern that he hath upon his mind for a considerable time past, to pay a religious Visit to the Meeting of Friends within the compass of your Quarterly meeting, and requested a certificate :

We do therefore certify, that we have Unity with him, as a Member and Minister, and with this his intended Visit. We recommend him to your brotherly care and regard and remain

Your Friends

Signed in and on behalf of Sedbergh Monthly Meeting held at Garsdale the 26th of 4th mo 1791

David Harker	John Hunter	Anthony Mason
	Richard Hodgson	Thos. Carter
	Jer. Thistlethwaite	John Holme

Tho Greenwood	Edward Smith
Robert Jackson	Edmond Winn
John Moore	Simon Harker
John Wilkinson	John Ion
Richard Wilkinson	Matthew Middlebrook
John Bradley	Rob Foster
	John Atkinson
	Joshua Smith (7)

It is of particular interest to us, in the day when some churches are still considering the ministry of women, that 300 years ago the Quakers received the ministry of women equally with that of men.

From time to time a cautionary, or even discordant, note is struck. On the 26th of August 1715 it was desired that Friends:

'be constrained in stiring up those that sit near them that they see overcome with sleepiness'

No doubt the long days of work, the keeness of the dale's air and the silence of the meeting overcame the most willing. A dozen years later we read :

'Friends is concerned to advise to plainness and against needless facions some is ready to follow'

and a minute of the Kendal quarterly meeting of 1706 is quoted in full as authoritative. After an appeal to 'our holy prefession of truth of Christianity which leads into humility and plainness' the superfluous fashions of the world which are to be avoided are described :

'wide sleued mantes with short and longe laps and knoting of handcirchefs in a superflues manner for preventing of which it is desired that frinds would pin them down to cover their stomigrs & laces Yt is allso desired that frids wold weare their Aperell of a grave coulours & plin in their head drisses without so many needless nips & peaks haveing their clothes fast to their heads that their hare be not seen' (8)

It is not only the women who are advised against superfluity. A minute of 1711 from Brigflatts reads :

'Several Friends being uneasy to see so many amongst us have cutt of their hair and gott wiggs which hath formerly been advised against, this meeting to prevent superfluities concludes ... that none amongst Friends doe cutt of their hair & wear a wigg untill they have first made the preparative meeting they belong to sensible there is a necessity for it' (9)

Even more seriously in the 1730's there creep into the Grisdale/Garsdale minutes admonitions delivered to young Quaker women in the families of the valley, as, for example, 'thing that is needful hath been spoken to Jane Dawson' (on July 22nd 1731 and July 23rd 1732). Similar words were spoken to Mary Harker on the 25th of November 1731, to Isabel Alderson on October 26th 1733 and Rebeckan Fathergill on October 27th 1733.

It is obvious that the words spoken were about marriage out of the society. Both the young men and women of the society found the stringent regulations (that they should marry within Quaker families only) hard to bear, and they were looking elsewhere. Unfortunately Jane Dawson died while still young and was buried at Scale in 1737.

Soon after that date, in 1748, John Griffiths, a travelling minister for the Quakers, recorded in his Journal :

'Next day I had a very comfortable reviving meeting among a few plain friends in Grisdale'

At this point we turn our attention to the Grisdale/Garsdale Men's affairs. There are several minute books beginning in 1740. Inside the back cover of the first book is written :

'This Book was begun by Adam Harker then Clerk to the meeting afterwards Robert Akerigg was Clerk and this Book was finished the year 1754 by John Wilkinson' (10)

Adam Harker built Low Scale (Garsdale) in 1723, Robert Harker lived at Aldershaw, Grisdale, which was rebuilt in 1775 by Robert Akrigg, and John Wilkinson lived at Knudmanning. He was born in 1722 and died in 1822, unless there is some confusion in the records. His mother was Janet Sutton (1677-1743) whose ministry before her marriage we have noticed. Inside the front cover of the book is written twice : 'Jannet Wilkinson'. It is written first in the handwriting of John Wilkinson and then in a shakier copy:

Was this 'underwriting'? Perhaps the mother copied her name some time before her death, or was it John's daughter, also Jannet, who was not born till 1760, who copied it as a child?

The pressure exerted on Quaker young people by strict marriage requirements can be seen in the strange entry in the Brigflatts monthly meeting minutes for the 28th of the 4th month of 1761 :

'Thomas Close and Richard Thistlet(hwaite) gave account they answered the appt in attending Garstal Meeting and found that a Young Man not of our profession and Agness Ackrigg (of our Society) had some sort of clandestine marriage and by circumstances that appear they break into the Meeting House to perform the same'. (11)

She could well have been the sister of the man who built Aldershaw 14 years later and we may imagine the perturbation of spirit which made a Quaker girl, and her lover, break into the meeting house because she felt that the marriage would not be blessed unless it was performed there, even if the congregation were absent. In 1771 a Robert Akrig married a woman 'of a different persuasion' and was disowned. Was he the one who built Aldershaw in 1775, or was he his son? When a Robert Akrig was buried at Scale in 1815 he was described as 'not in unity'. Certainly the story gives added poignancy to to a reference in the monthly meeting Book of Disownments where we read : (12)

'Whereas Richard Wilkinson Son of John Wilkinson of Garsdale & Katharine his Wife by birthright a member of our Society, for want of taking heed to the divine principle placed in every heart (which if duely regarded would preserve from evil) & contrary to the timely and repeated cautions & advice of his relations and friends persisted in keeping company with a Young woman not of our Society with whom he had been guilty of fornication & aterwards marrying by Priest.

We therefore believe it our duty to give forth this public testimony against such reproachful & inconsistent Conduct, & do hereby disown the said Richd Wilkinson from membership with us yet Desiring that it may before it be too late become sensible of his Outgoings & by sincere Repentance & conversion obtain forgiveness.

Signed on behalf of Sedbergh
Monthly meeting, held at Lee Yeat in
Dent the 27th of 9th mo 1790 by Tho Harter Clerk'

We may imagine the sadness of Quaker parents that such indictments should be recorded against their children. This also account for the tone of a 'testimony' left by John Wilkinson, as clerk to the meeting, about his wife who died about the time of their ruby wedding :

'I have a testimony to Give of my late Loveing Wife Katherine Wilkinson that she was a Loveing and Faithful

I have this Testimony to Give of my late Loveing Wife Katharine Wilkinson that She was a loveing and faithfull Wife to me and fully Performed her Marriage Covenant a Loveing tender and Affectionate mother to her Children and often Concerned for their good an industris and Frugal Wife yet open hearted (Charitable) and Delighted in doing good to all a frequent visiter of the Sick. a Sincere Lover and Promoter of Peace: a Diligent attender of meetings when in health (and often invited me to go with her when I did not to my now deep Sorrow) She was endued with abundance of Patience which helped her through many hard trials and Continued Patient and Perfectly Sensible to the last and Quietly Departed this Life (I believe in Peace) without Sigh or Groan like one falling asleep the nineteenth day of the Third month 1796 in the Sixty-third year of her age

John Wilkinson

John Wilkinson's Testimony to his wife; and a 'disownment' notice in the Book of Disownments.

Sarah Greenwood :: A Member of our Society having been married in a manner contrary to our rules, was thereupon visited when she acknowledged to the truth thereof, We therefore to testify our dis approbation of such conduct here-by disunite the said Sarah Greenwood now Mackereth from Membership with us.

Signed in and on behalf of Sedbergh Monthly Meeting held at Brigflatts the 28 of 1st Month 1823 by ————

Thomas Harker

Clerk

Wife to me and fully Performed her marriage covenant a Loveing tender and Affectionate mother to her Children and often concerned for their Good an industrus and Frugal Wife yet open hearted Charitable and Delighted in doing Good to all, a frequent visitor of the sick, a Sincere Lover and Promoter of Peace a Diligent attender of meetings when in health (and often invited me to go with her when I did not to my deep sorrow) She was endued with abundance of Patience which helped her through many hard trials and continued Patient and Perfectly sensible to the last and Quietly departed this Life (I believe in peace) without a sigh or a Groan like one falling asleep the nineteenth day of the third month 1796 in the sixty-third year of her age.

John Wilkinson' (13)

The second volume of the Men's minutes was begun on the 26th of the 1st month 1754 and goes on to the 23rd of the 12th month 1792. There is more of business matters in the Men's books, as, for example, in the autumn of 1754 when a tenfold collection was requested to help in the enlargement of the Ravenstonedale meeting house. It amounted to £1:16:2. Two years later the yearly meeting was to be held at Penrith and preparations had to be made. The men were asked to subscribe :

'towards building ashade at Penrith for the accomodation of the next yearly meeting'

If we interpret 'shade' in the Oxford dictionary sense of 'a retired spot' we shall see why soon after 17 shillings was given 'towards making convenience at Penrith'.

In 1765 consideration was given to the repair of the meeting house in Grisdale and following was minuted:

'It was agreed by friends in Grisdale to give sums of money following for the repair of the meeting house in Grisdale that is to say

Thomas Winn	1: 1:	0
Michael Akerigg	15:	0
Samuel Lund	10:	0
Joshua Alderson	5:	0
Thomas Alderson	5:	0'

The will of Thomas Winn was made on February 19th 1775, and proved on May 24th 1777. He left £40, but the burial record says of him 'He was an Ancient valuable Publick Friend'. He lived long enough to see his son, Edmond, return to the Quaker fold for, on 22nd of November 1776 the minutes state :

'Edmond Winn of Grisdale haveing signified his desire to be reunited with Friends therefore Edmond Winn and Simon Harker are appointed by this meeting the visit him and give account of how they think of his worthiness'

By the end of the year John Wilkinson was helping him to prepare a submission in writing for the monthly meeting.

Sons of families still figure in the book : John Raw was, in 1778, reprimanded for 'misconduct', and Joshua Alderson was, in 1781, reported as having been 'married by a priest'. There were complaints that the meetings were not so well attended as they might have been, and, the spring of 1788 another attempt was made to repair the Grisdale meeting room:

> 'This meeting appoints William Hodgson, Simon Harker and John Wilkinson to see what Friends in Grisdale and Garsdale will subscribe towards repairing the Meeting House in Grisdale and also to make an estimate of the expense and assist in forwarding the work'

A month later the reply came back that the Grisdale Friends 'proposed to repair said Meeting House at their own expense'.

A further book was begun in January 1793 which concluded in December 1828. The last book began in January 1829 and ended the series in October 1848. John Wilkinson is the first scribe of the last book. A new generation had taken over.

From 1836 the majority of the meetings were held at Garsdale and for many months no births, burials or removals were recorded. In 1837 the birth of Isabella Davis is mentioned, and birth notes were given for the daughters of John Lund : Betty, Agnes and Mary.

As the 1840's dawned there were a series of burials culminating in that of Elizabeth Akrigg of Aldershaw who was buried on the 6th of August 1843. We reproduce the official request to the grave maker, James Blades.

David Butler (14) states that the closure of the Grisdale meeting was about 1870 and was connected with a revival of work in Garsdale. There is no sign of this from the Preparative Meeting minute book, but it does record attempts to influence the people of the two dales. It states that on the 25th October 1844:

> 'Our friend James Backhouse of York was at a publick meeting in Garsdale and one in Grisdale on the 31st both of them was well attended'

James Backhouse also came to Grisdale in 1845 and 1848, when the last entry in the book is :

> 'were this day Favoured with the company of our Friends James Backhouse and Thomas Handley at meeting in Grisdale'

The handwriting, at this point, quavers to a stop and 'the rest is silence'.

THE MEETING IN GRISDALE

The Sedbergh monthly meeting in 1886 reported on Grisdale :

> 'The Meeting House is used by the Wesleyans at a rent of 5/- per annum (a footnote adds '10/-p.a., 5/- allowed for repairs') but they are getting tired of it as it is old & out of repair & and contemplate building a place of worship for themselves...To patch the place up seems out of the question, to rebuild seems rather like a waste of money, & to sell seems objectionable' (15)

In 1860 a local man recorded that 'the beck was in flood and the floor was all swimming'.

What happened to the build we shall record when we consider the story of the Methodist society.

. . . . .

1: Copy of Conveyance. Loose papers : Cumbria Record Office, Kendal. WDFC F
2: Brigflatts yearly meeting : CRO, Kendal WDFC F.
3: Grisdale/Garsdale Women's Preparative Meeting minutes CRO Kendal : WDFC F
4: Kendal Quarterly meeting minutes : CRO Kendal WDFC F
5: Sedbergh Monthly Meeting minutes, loose papers CRO Kendal WDFC F
6: Grisdale/Garsdale Women's Preparative Meeting minutes CRO Kendal. WDFC F.
7: Sedbergh Monthly Meeting minutes, as above.
8: Kendal Quarterly Meeting minutes, as above.
9: Brigflatts Monthly Meeting minutes : CRO Kendal. WDFC F.
10: Grisdale/Garsdale Men's Preparative Meeting minutes. CRO, Kendal WFCF F.
11: as 9.
12: Book of Disownments CRO Kendal WDFC F
13: Loose papers Sedbergh, as 5.
14: David Butler : Quaker Meeting Houses of the Lake Counties Friends Historical Society, London 1978.
15: Norman Penney 'Narrative of Friends Mission in Hawes and Wensleydale' 1882-6. MSS Friends House Library, London.

To Friends of the Quarterly Meeting of Durham

Dear Friends.

John Laycock the bearer hereof, having laid before us a concern, that he hath had upon his mind for a considerable time past, to pay a religious visit to the Meetings of Friends within the compass of your Quarterly Meeting, & requested a Certificate:

We do therefore certify, that we have Unity with him as a member & Minister, & with this his intended Visit. We recommend him to your brotherly care & regard herein.

Your Friends

Signed in & on behalf of Sedbergh Monthly Meeting held at Garsdale the 26th of 4m: 1791

David Harker

John Hunter
Richard Hodgson
Jer. Thistlethwaite

Tho. Greenwood

Robert Jackson
John Moore
John Wilkinson
Richard Wilkinson
John H Bradley

Anthony Mason
Thos Carter
John Holme
Edward Smith
Edmond Winn
Simon Harker
John Ton
Matthew Middlebrook
Rob Foster
John Atkinson
Joshua Smithson

A Certificate given to John Laycock for a ministerial visit to Durham.

48

THE HOUSES OF THE DALE

The silent, often ruined, houses of the dale cannot tell us who built them, or when they were built, and there is not much external evidence to help us find out. Only one of the houses carries a dated stone, as houses in Garsdale sometimes do, and though the familiar names of today's houses appear in early indentures this refers to the farm rather than to the buildings which stood on it. Often the buildings on a farm are listed in the indenture, as for example, an indenture of 1735 which lists 'a dwelling-house, a hay-house, a stable, a cow-house, and a peat house'. Among the building so mentioned is usually 'house', but occasionally 'mansion'. It is tempting to think that the man who re-built his house in the fine style which survives to this day might proudly refer to it as a 'mansion', but we cannot be sure. It was probably just a form of words.

The charters of the monks of Jervaulx abbey included permission from their donating lords to take timber from the forest in order to build the monastery buildings and it is safe to assume that the earliest houses, even in an area like Grisdale, where timber is not plentiful, would be built of timber frames and wattle and mud walls. Celia Fiennes travelled through the Lake District in 1698 and commented :

> 'you pass by the little Hutts and hovels the poor live in like barnes some have them daub'd with mud-wall others drye wall'. (1)

and she comments on the 'sadd little Hutts' near Windermere. These were the houses of the poor and it is interesting to ask if the distinction between 'mudd-wall' and 'drye' refers to the dry-stone walling techniques which survive to this day? If this is so such walls would need to be mud plastered inside to limit the penetration of the persistent wind. This appears to have been done in what survives of Viking summer houses on the slopes of Ribblehead.

Celia Fiennes was quite capable of making meaningful comparisons between the housing of the poor and that of the rich for she had passed through 'Wiggons' (Wigan) and called it, 'a pretty market town built of stone and brick', and she remarked that Kendal was built all of stone. Indeed she took any opportunity she could of visiting stately homes and described them in glowing terms.

It does not seem possible that most of those who took over the valley after the monastic period would ever be among the 'poor', and the frugality and industry of the early Quakers would mean that they were not more laggard than their neighbours in improving their homes for themselves and their families.

What surviving examples there are of medieval houses in other parts of the country suggest that the family home was based on a common hall with a central hearth. From this the smoke sought to escape through louvres set in the apex of the roof and by an other means available to it. There was little privacy in such a house and only the master and mistress might have a separate bedroom, and, even there, the children or servants would sleep on truckle beds. In such an atmosphere our 'kippered' ancestors lived, and probably did not wash too often in any case. When the chance came for the Quaker people, who had a reputation for clean linen, they would change all that. The central hearth gave way first to a wood and plaster vent, which Celia Fiennes calls 'a tunnell', and then, those who could afford them built houses with proper chimneys such as had graced the warming rooms of the monasteries for centuries.

These houses would consist first of 'the house', 'house-place' or 'fire-house', which was the living room of the family. To this was added a parlour, a kitchen and buttery, as 'outshuts', and an inside staircase which led to divided bedrooms upstairs. To this day in the dale there are houses where you pass from one bedroom to another rather than the later method of access by a common corridor. As stone was the most readily available material locally these houses were built of stone. It was also a most enduring material and some of them have stood for more than 300 years. In the roof spaces of many of these buildings the timbers speak volumes of how trees were adapted to carry the load. I have seen a roughly squared tree trunk holding an upper floor with the branch fork kept, in order to attain the length needed to reach the further wall. The medieval monk's dormatory in Durham has a similar feature.

Only three houses in the valley have been continuously occupied: Blakemire, Mouse Syke and East House. No doubt they, since their first rebuilding in stone, have been modified and improved. Aldershaw has been rebuilt from a ruinous state and Moor Rigg has been divided into three houses. Other houses, such as Feafow, are being rescued from ruin. At East and West Scale the roofs survive though the houses have been empty since the early years of the century.

Chapelhouse was built in 1889 as a Wesleyan chapel in memory of Richard Atkinson to whom we shall return later. Beck House was a 'laithe', or field house, for the Moor Rigg and Mouse Syke farms. 'Becks' as a new area for Mouse Syke is found in an indenture of 1738 but no barn is mentioned, so it was probably built after the field was taken over. When it was converted into a house we had the opportunity to examine closely the manner of building. The stone layers of the inner skin of the wall were laid regularly with attention being paid to neatness and style. The outer stone wall was 'water-shot'. That means

The roof timbers of Fea Fow; and the shippon behind old Mouse Syke.

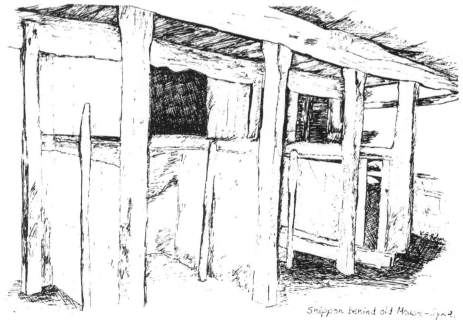

that the stones were so laid that the inner edge of the stone is about three inches higher than the outside edge with the result that water striking the building would naturally drain away down the wall rather than penetrate it. There is nothing random or casual about the buildings of the valley.

It is said that the population of the valley declined to its present state because of a succession of bad winters before the second world war, but a passage in The Friend for July 16th 1920 suggests that the rot had set in much earlier than that. A visitor to the dale remarked on the absence of a school or post office and said that the Quaker burial ground had not been used for fifty years. The landlord wished to sell the farms but the tenants did not have the money to buy.

In the light of all this is there any way we can give a date to these silent stones?

One way of reaching a date would be to see what was happening in surrounding areas. In a recent article by M.E. Garnett (2) the author traces 420 lintel stones in South Lonsdale dated between 1600 and 1730. In Garsdale, which was intimately connected with Grisdale by family ties and common worship, there is a lintel stone at Swarthgill which reads IHI 1712. It was the home of John Haygarth (1674-1757) and the first I (or J) was for John, and the second for his wife, Isabell. Their famous grandson, Dr John Haygarth M.D. F.R.S was born at Swarthgill. At Low Scar, further up the valley, we find ID:ID 1724. Perhaps this stone recalls the Dawson family. The mullioned windows there, and elsewhere in the dale, were put in, it is suggested, to demonstrate that the builder had wealth.

Even higher up Garsdale, in the living room at Low Scale, is a salt or spice cupboard built into the wall which reads H A E 1723. The H is for Harker, and the A and E for Adam and Emma. Adam Harker of Swaledale married Emma Wilkinson of Knudmanning in 1703. We shall have reason to return to the Harkers for in 1709 Emma's sister, Jane, married Michael Dawson of Grisdale, a Quaker. When she died in 1736 she left £5 for the repair of the meeting house in Garsdale.

There are only two dated lintels in Grisdale. One is on a barn near Aldershaw and is dated 1885. It is said to be the last building erected in the valley before the chapel in 1889. In Aldershaw itself there is a lintel dated 1775 with the letter A above the date, and R and E on the left and right of it. This must be Robert and Elizabeth Akrigg. Elizabeth was buried at Scale in 1781, where Robert followed her in 1815 aged 83, and is decribed as 'of Aldershaw'. This means that he must have been 43 when he and his wife built the house though she was to die soon after. Both Robert and Elizabeth were said to be 'not in unity' with the Quakers, though they were buried in the Quaker burial ground. For this reason neither their marriage, nor the births of their children, appear in the Quaker records.

spice cupboard door

Things were happening in the dales. It was a time of peace and prosperity and agricultural improvement. The people had money to spare. Even small groups built for themselves: the deeds of the Old Police House in Garsdale say that it was originally built as a chapel by 14 'Congregational Persuasionists'. Everyone took his chance.

All these dates would fit into a similar pattern to that of South Lonsdale, and we have no need to assume that the Grisdale Quakers were slower or less capable of re-building than their neighbours and relatives in Garsdale. Just how close was the inter-relationship between families of the two dales may be seen by a glance at the marriage records kept by the Quakers. In 1686 the marriage of Edmond Winn and Agnes Regnoldson was announced in the minutes of the Brigflatts meeting, both fathers being present and consenting. It took place on the 2nd day of the 5th month 1687. Within two years the two sisters of Agnes had married in to Quaker families : Mary married Michael

Dawson on the 5th day of the second month, 1688; and Alice married John Hodgson on the 9th day of the 3rd month 1700. This brought together the Winns, the Regnoldsons, the Dawsons and the Hodgsons. In 1689 Thomas Winn married Ann Harker of Swaledale (on the 12th of the 3rd), and in 1703 her brother, Adam, married Emma Wilkinson (on the 18th of the 3rd). If we add to this that in 1709 Jane Wilkinson married Thomas Close the threads were becoming even more entangled, for it was John Close, the father of John Close Junior, who inherited half the land of the first Quaker Winn, Reynold, in 1677. These links could be taken further, but the point is made. (3)

Kevin Lancaster in the Sedbergh Historian refers to the:

> 'disputes between the Strickland Family, Lords of the Manor of Sedbergh, and the Freeeholders of the district as recorded in the Dalton Bluecaster papers which came to light earlier this year' (1989). (4)

These disputes began in 1704 and continued through the 1730's and were about who had the right to mine stone, and stone slate (as well as coal), on Baugh Fell. Previous to 1700 the houses of the dales had been built of 'undressed stone covered in thatch'. Those who held tenements had been allowed to take such random stone by their Deeds of Enfranchisment granted from the Strickland Manor between 1616 and 1620. Here was a further opportunity, thought the holders, and an improved one at that.

Mr Lancaster dates the discovery of sandstone slate on Baugh Fell at about 1690 and gives the evidence, which is not our concern. The rest of the story is of the to and fro of legal argument as to who should benefit from the quarrying of stone and slate in an area which overlooks Grisdale. Whatever was the right or wrong of the legal argument without doubt the land-holders of Grisdale, and Garsdale, must have taken the opportunity offered to obtain stone, and stone slates, to rebuild their houses. In this way the dates of between 1700 and 1730 seen on the lintels of the Garsdale houses could have been paralleled in Grisdale if the builders of the houses had taken their chisels into their hands.

I was asked by a visitor to the dale if I knew the significance of the cairns which top Grisdale Pike below Baugh Fell brow. Were they signs of early man, or were they put there to guide the wandering shepherd? It is said that a chambered tomb was once discovered at Seaty Hill, Malham, in which the skeleton of a fully dressed Celtic chief sits looking at just such a cairn as those on Grisdale Pike. Did such cairns have a ritual significance? I think the answer could be much simpler. Those who quarried the stone slate threw aside broken pieces and either they, needing guide posts to the quarries in bad weather, or later visitors, wanting to leave a mark on the landscape, built a memorial to their passing.

It seems that, in the period of prosperity which followed the accession of Charles II in 1660, those who shared that prosperity, and the confidence it brought, were not slow to rebuild their houses in fine style, and, as we have seen, put their initials and a date on some of the lintel stones. This would be typical of the yeomen, the 'statesmen', of the dales, secure in their tenure and working hard and growing prosperous. It may be that a man had inherited an unencumbered estate from his father, he had married, as Adam Harker did in 1703, and carefully paid off the legacies with which his father had burdened the estate. His family soon grew to the point when they could add to the common income. Adam Harker's family did just this since Mary, Emme, John, Margrett and Richard were born between 1704 and 1713. Ten years after the birth of his last child, and while he might anticipate fifteen or more years of life, was the time to renew his house. Perhaps he would borrow the £100 it would cost and pay it off in the remaining years of his working life. Adam Harker was lucky, for he lived another thirty years, both he and his wife dying in 1755.

· · · · ·

1 : Celia Fiennes : The Illustrated Journeys of Celia Fiennes c 1682-1712 ed Christopher Morris. First published in Great Britain in 1982 by Webb and Bower (Publishers) Ltd.

2 : M.E. Garnett : 'The great rebuilding in South Lonsdale, 1600 to 1730'. Transactions of the Historic Society of Lancashire and Cheshire. 1988.

3 : Quaker Dates : In 1752 the Gregorian calendar was adopted which eliminated the 11 day error of the Julian calendar and changed New Year's Day from March 25th to January 1st. The Quakers, however, never accepted the 'pagan' names used by us (January after Janus, March after Mars etc) and prefered to call the months 'first month' 'second month' and so on. Before 1752 for the Quakers March was 'first month' and February was 'twelfth month'. I have left the dates in general as the Quakers expressed them with this (all too simple) explanation. For a fuller explanation see : Isobel Ross : Margaret Fell (2nd edition 1984), notes on pp vi to viii by Edward H. Mulligan and Malcolm J. Thomas.

4 : Kevin Lancaster : The Sedbergh Historian, Vol 2 No 4 Spring 1989.

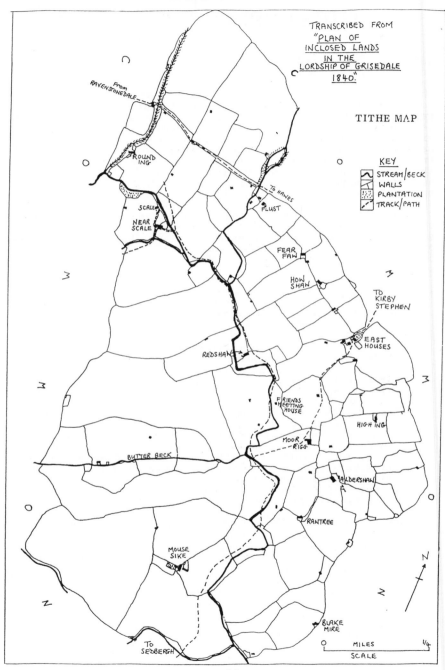

TRANSCRIBED FROM
"PLAN OF
INCLOSED LANDS
IN THE
LORDSHIP OF GRISEDALE
1840."

TITHE MAP

KEY
STREAM/BECK
WALLS
PLANTATION
TRACK/PATH

From
RAVENSTONEDALE

ROUND
ING

To HAWES

SCALE

FLUST

NEAR
SCALE

FEAR
FAW

HOW
SHAN

TO
KIRBY
STEPHEN

EAST
HOUSES

REDSHAW

FRIENDS
MEETING
HOUSE

HIGH ING

MOOR
RIGG

BUTTER BECK

ALDERSHAW

RANTREE

MOUSE
SIKE

N

BLAKE
MIRE

To
SEDBERGH

MILES
SCALE
1/4

THE PEOPLE OF THE DALE

One of the difficulties we have in learning about the silent people of the valley is that they left few, or no, personal documents behind them. The best we have are the wills they made. We shall look at those wills which survive from this period and see how the testators thought about their earthly treasures, and how they reacted to the prospect of eternity. We shall also consider some of the artefacts left from the time, and those mentioned in inventories, and see how their silence speaks.

The will of Reynold Winn is typical, and particularly interesting. A copy of it is in the registry of wills in the Lonsdale deanery kept at Preston, together with the certificate of authentification, signed by John Close, one of the beneficiaries, on the seventh of December 1677. Here is the will :

'June 4th. In the name of God Amen. I Reynold Winn of Grisdale weake in body but in prfect mind and memorye, praised be God, doe make this my laste will and testament in maner and forme as followeth :

Imprimis I doe give to my wife Mabell Winn halfe of all my goods, excepting cupboards, bedstocks, tables and bords, they may remain in the houses untill the death of my wife, and then to goe with the houses and grounds to them it is ordered for.

Item I give twentie pounds to be let forthe and the profett of it everie yeare shall goe to the maintaineinge of a schoole master in Grisedale and att any time when their is no schoole master kept in Grisdale for that time the yearely proffits shall goe to the Poore of Grisdale and Garsdale and I apoint George Winn and Michell Dawson the elder and Michaell Dawson the youngest to be ffeoffers in truste for the same and when any of them dies the other shall take another to them and so to continue for ever.

Item I give to Ralfe Metcalfe wife my brother John Winn daughter ten pounds. Item I give to Gilbert Guy wife my brother John daughter ten pounds. Item I give to Elizabeth Winn my brother John daughter twentie pounds Item I give to Margarett Winn my brother John daughter twenty pounds. Item I give to John Burrow twenty shillings Item I give to Alice Burroes twenty shillings Item I give to Edward Burrow twentie shillings Item I give to Margrett Burrow thre pound Item I give to Marygrett Close thre pounds Item I give to Mabell Close two pounds Item I give to Barnard Atkinson twenty shillings Item I give to Issabell Shawe

Edmond Shawe wife twentie shillings Item I give to James
Adamthwaite ten shillings Item I give to Mabell my
maidservant one ten out of the whole Item I give to Henry
Shawe wife ten shillings Item I give to Elizabeth Shaw
Thomas Shaw daughter ten shillings Item I give to Miles
Shawe ten shillings Item I give to Issabell Shawe ten
shillings Item I give to Agnes Shaw younger ten shillings
Item I give to Thomas Johnson wife John Fothergill
daughter ten shillings Item I give my manservant George
Dent ten shillings Item I give to George Winn five pounds
Item I give to Thomas Burrow one pound Item I give to
Brian Nelson and also James Nelson sons of John Nelson
either of them ten shillings Item all the rest of my goods
undisposed of if their be any syne it to John Close and I
doe make him my whole executor of this my last will and
testament. And I apoint my brother John Winn Antony Mason,
Renold Harrison and Edmond Winn executors of this my will
to see it performed and I doe give them twentie shillings
a peece out of the whole.
      Witness my hand'   (1)

It will be noted that Reynold Winn was generous, but he was
also wealthy. At a time when other wills showed that people
died possessed of not more than £20 or £40 he left £167 with
much more than that due to him. It is also of interest that he
left provision for a schoolmaster in the valley. We do not know
for certain where Reynold Winn was buried. His name does not
appear in the parish registers, but it was sometimes the
practice for Quakers to bury in their own grounds. The Quaker
burial ground record at Scale gives the first burial as that of
Abraham Dent on the 7th of the 12th month in 1679, two years
after Reynold Winn's death. It seems, from other records, that
Reynold Winn may have lived at Scale, in which case it is also
possible that he gave the ground for the burial place and is,
himself, buried there.

Like most of the people in our story Reynold Winn is more
shadowy than we could wish. Perhaps converted by Fox in 1652,
protesting against tithes in 1660, appearing as a witness in a
number of wills , and a 'pricer' in others, he finally left us
his will in 1677. I wish we knew more. There are two small
documents which shed light on him. On September 8th 1674
'Katheren' Dawson asked him to write out her will dividing her
small property, worth £29:13:4 between her two sons, Robert and
Richard. This he did, and witnessed it, but omitted to get a
second witness to the document. When she died it appears that
the will was questioned because he was the only witness. With
her will is a letter of explanation which, like the will, is in
his handwriting. I reproduce both on the opposite page, and add
here a transcription :

    'these are to certifie unto all thouse it may concerne
that Katheren late wife of Michael Dawson of Grisdale did
send for me and I did writ hir mind I remember it was in

September the 8: 1675

In the name of god amen I Katheren Dawson being in perfect mind and memorie prayse be god do make this my last will and testament in maner and forme as followeth & I comit my soule to all mighty god my maker and redemer and my bodye to be buried in the church or church yard of Garsdale

Item I give to my son Robert Dawson forte shillinges that I lent him and liveteen 12 pounds that I lent to him or his son michell Dawson and a cubart and a bed and one chist

Item I give to my son Richard Dawson tho ten pound that I have owing in Wensedale

Item I give to Katheren Dawson wife Robert Dawson dowther all the rest of my houshould goods

Item I give to my son Robert and Richard all the rest of my goods or money not disposed of & they to be my sole executors of this my last will and testament and it is my mind and will that Robert and Richard my two sones shall pay all charges for my bringing forth and to bring me honestly forth

witnes my hand

witnessed heere
Reynold Winn

KATHEREN DAWSON'S WILL, written out by Reynold Winn,
and his explanatory letter.

These are to certefie unto all whome it may concerne that Katheren Dawson late wife of michell Dawson of ... Syde did send for mee and I did write her mind ... I remember it was in september three yeares and she did send for me two yeares after and I did reed unto it over and she well satisfyed with it and this last time said it should never be altered ... I leaved no moment present but my love to you and in hast rest

witnes my hand, Reynold Winn

(Garsdale october)
the 25: 1675

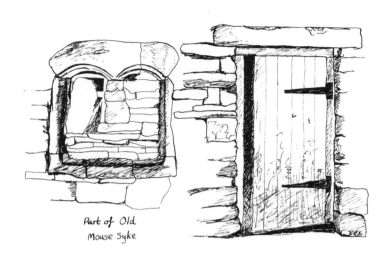

Part of Old
Mouse Syke

hay knife

September three yeares since and she did send for me tow
severall times and I did reed hir it ower and she was well
satisfied with it and the last time said it should never
be altered no more at present but my love to you and in
hast rest

                              Witness my hand Reynold Winn
Grisdale October
the 25th 1677   (2)

By December of the same year Reynold Winn himself was dead.
He had done his last service to his old friend, Michael Dawson
his fellow Quaker, his wife Katherine and their two boys. We do
not know his age, but the effort it cost him may be seen in the
handwriting.

M.E. Garnett imagines the end of the statesman's story:

'If he lived long enough he ultimately pensioned himself
off, retiring into one or two rooms, keeping a couple of
beasts in the family herd and riding his pony, and living
quietly on the interest of his capital'. (3)

So the children, or more likely the grand-children, of men
like Reynold Winn re-built the houses of the dale and recorded
on the death of their neighbours what those houses contained.
The fact that one house in Grisdale today carries a date of
1775 does not mean that all the houses that remain are as late
as that, or that no mysteries remain. East House is, in early
documents called 'East Houses', and behind Mouse Syke there is
a building, which is now a barn, some of the stones of which
could be described as 'Elizabethan'. Moreover, one document of
1738 refers to two houses at Mouse Syke. Why is this, and where
do those seemingly earlier stones come from? Perhaps the
present house at Mouse Syke replaced the earlier house which
was turned into a barn. It is also hard to resist the thought
that some features of one or two other houses in the dale, like
the circular staircases at West Scale and Feafow are, like the
barn windows at Mouse Syke, 'Elizabethan' in style and either
represent a throw-back to an earlier style of building or a re-
use of older stone. Perhaps even more likely is the possibility
that when older houses were re-built parts of the former house
(like the solid circular staircases) were incorporated into the
newer building. It would have been a major task to move them.

Built into one or two of the barns of the valley are carved
stones, some as lintels, but others simply placed at random
into the walls. Could those hard-working Quakers, who believed
in simplicity, and who had little time or money to spare, have
solemnly sat down to carve decorated stones simply to set them
at random into a barn wall? It is inconceivable. Are we,
perhaps, looking at material brought from elsewhere, even,
maybe, from a monastic house, which was being reused? We shall
never know.

Detail of Howshaw
Barn.

West Scale.

THE PEOPLE OF THE DALE

All the records available to us, the birth registers and, from 1841, the census returns, suggest that families were large and it could not have been easy for so small an area to support large numbers. There were once nearly forty children who went to school, first at Reacher, and then over the top to Lunds in Mallerstang. Indentures which survive show that land was being bought and sold all the time, but even so every family had a means of support other than farming. They were farmers; but they were also hosiers like Reynold Winn, and there were butchers, blacksmiths, coal miners, shoemakers and quarrymen and other occupations.

A visit to the Upper Dales Folk Museum housed in the old railway buildings at Hawes is the best introduction to life and work in the upland dales of long ago for those who have never known anything but tractors, motor cars and the land-buggies of today. There artefacts, lovingly collected by Marie Hartley and Joan Ingilby, not only show the contents of a dalesman's house but how work on the land was carried out in former days. There are yokes and back-cans for carrying milk, and cheese and butter making utensils. There, too, are hay sweeps, peat barrows and spades, scythes, and drenching horns and many other things not used today. They enable us to look at the yearly round of the dale : ploughtime (where there was arable land), tupping time, lambing time, turf time and haytime. Such a life has not changed much over the centuries except that modern machinery enables the hard work to be done by one man rather than by many.

When we look at the household effects in the museum we realise how sparsley furnished were their homes compared with ours, and those objects clothe with meaning the inventory entries we find in the wills which we quote here and in the chapter on the Scale burial ground.

Most of the wills conclude with an inventory of the owner's property in which items of furniture are valued. To return to the will of Reynold Winn (1677) we read that when his goods were valued on December 1st 1677 they were :

Inpr :	His apparall rideinge ffurniture and money in the house	£69 :	17 :	0
Itm	Bedding and bedstocks	2 :	10 :	0
Itm	Brasse and Pewter	1 :	0 :	0
Itm	Wood vessell	1 :	0 :	0
Itm	Fire vessell	1 :	0 :	0
Itm	Tables, chists, chaires, and stools	1 :	10 :	0
Itm	Cupboard and Dishbench	1 :	0 :	0
Itm	Meale Butter Cheese and Beefe	3 :	6 :	8
Itm	Wooll and Stockings	6 :	15 :	0
Itm	Husbandry geare and peats		13 :	4
Itm	Haye	8 :	0 :	0
Itm	7 kine one heffer and a Bull	26 :	0 :	0
Itm	Nine young beasts	12 :	0 :	0

Itm	1 Mare and fillie		5 : 10 : 0
Itm	Weathers	29	10 : 0 : 0
Itm	Ewes	45	11 : 0 : 0
Itm	Hogs	33	6 : 10 : 0
			-----------
			167 : 12 : 0
	Due to the Dect by Specialty		394 : 17 : 4
	without Specialty		40 : 9 : 4

	Ex Sub Ptestr Som tot		602 : 18 : 8
			-----------

and even if the values were 'written down' for legal reasons
they seem to have taken to heart the injunction that 'man's
life does not consist in the abundance of the things that he
possesseth'. A 'hog', it should be noted, is a female sheep
under a year old which has not yet had a lamb.

The fact that we see references to 'bedstocks' as a treasure
to hand on to the family is a silent witness to the fact that
the servants, and perhaps others, slept on the floor or on a
hay bolster at best. Everything of value appears on the
inventory which had to be 'priced' by four men 'sworn on the
book'.

Wensleydale is famous for its mild cheese and it may have
been made there since the days of Jervaulx Abbey, originally
out of ewe's milk. In Mouse Syke a shelf still exists in the
'house-place' for the drying and storing of cheese. Sheep were
the chief users of the high fells and those that had grown up
on a farm were usually sold with it because, if taken off the
land they knew, they would try to find their way back again. It
was in the local beck, suitably dammed, that the sheep were
washed and, ten days or so later, they were clipped. This was
usually a community occasion followed by a party. Lambing time
in Grisdale is usually in May when more and more white, and
wobbly, lambs appear which, as they gain confidence, run around
with their fellows.

Most people are familiar with the television programme 'One
man and his dog'. The present-day collie dog which can 'eye' a
sheep (that is control it with its eye) and 'sett' sheep lost
in a snow drift (that is locate them under many feet of snow)
is a relatively recent introduction from Scotland. Before the
collie was the rough, tough 'bearded dog' of the English breed,
the Old English sheep dog.

Early monastic charters gave rights of turbary, that is the
right to cut peat, as fuel for the monasteries. The right
became attached to the farms and, when the farm was sold, the
right went with it. Peat was cut after lambing time and stored
in peat houses. The road which winds over the hill from
Garsdale station to Dent is called 'the coal road'. Here are
many small pits from which coal was dug to mix with the peat.

Coal was also found on the slopes of Baugh Fell. Kevin Lancaster quotes Julia Green Vigour :

> 'The coal when procured was so slow burning that the morning fire lasted till afternoon - it was sulphrous and never blazes, though it burnt very red; to light it peat was wanted as well as wood' (4)

PEAT SPADE

We do not know at what stage the open fire with a 'reckan', or graduated spit holder, gave way to more modern ranges. In the Quaker period an iron pot with three legs would be suspended from the reckan and in this most things were boiled or baked. The baking was achieved by standing it on the fire on its three legs which allowed peats to be burned under it, and an iron lid allowed red hot peats to be heaped on top. Other essential equipment would be a spit, a broiling iron, dripping pans and chafing dishes. There would be no carpets, little glass and no knives and forks.

The staple diet of the dales was oatcake and this required a different method of cooking. Celia Fiennes, writing about 1698, described her first experience of eating it in Lancaster :

> 'Here I was first presented with clap bread which is much talked off made of oates; I was surprised when the cloth was laid they brought a great basket such as one uses to undress children with, and set it on the table full of thin wafers as big as a pancake and drye that they easily breake into shivers, but coming to dinner found it to be the only thing I must eate for bread, the taste of oate cake bread is pleasant enough and where it is well baked it is acceptable, but for the most part its scarce baked and full of drye flower on the outside'. (5)

A hundred years later William Wordsworth described how, on an excursion on the banks of Ullswater he stopped for food, and:

> 'The good woman treated us to oaten cakes new and crisp' (6)

In our area clap bread was called 'havercake' and was made from a thick dough rolled, or clapped, out on a board and cooked on a bakstone. This bakstone was a separate fire basket topped with thick slate under which a fire burned. Or the clap bread might be cooked on a circular iron plate suspended over the fire. Once cooked the oatcakes were hung over a 'flake' to dry until needed. Marie Hartley and Joan Ingilby write :

'Whenever it is mentioned people's eyes light up as they remember from their childhood the delicious smell on baking day, the well filled flake and the delectable taste of their favourite variety'.   (7)

An essential item of furniture would be the solid meal ark in which the oatmeal would be stored. This would be of oak, as would the cupboard for pewter, and some of the dishes. Clothes would be kept in chests or chists. These, with the tables and chairs would be handed on in their owner's will.

Adam Sedgwick of Dent gave a rosy picture of a dales family entertaining their neighbours. He wrote of :

'little family parties, who assembled together, in rotation, round one blazing fire, during the winter evenings....A Statesman's house in Dent had seldom more than two floors, and the upper floor did not extend to the wall where was the chief fire-place, but was wainscoted off from it. The consequence was, that part of the ground floor, near the fire-place was open to the rafters; which formed a wide pyramidal space, terminating in the principle chimney of the house. It was in this space, chiefly under the open rafters, that the family assembled.....about the end of the 17th century grates and regular flues began to be erected....they formed the exception and not the rule.

'A well-carved cupboard, or cabinet, marked with some date that fell within a period of fifty years after the restoration of Charles II'

Next let me shortly describe the furniture of this space where they held their evening 'sittings': First there was a blazing fire in a recess of a wall; which in the early times was composed of turf and great logs of wood. From one side of the fire-place was a bench, with a strong and sometimes ornamental carved back, called a lang settle. On the other side of the fire-place was the Patriarch's wooden and well-carved arm-chair; and near the chair was sconce adorned with crockery. Not far off was commonly

BECK HOUSE and CHAPEL HOUSE; and REACHER

Reacher

seen a well-carved cupboard, or cabinet, marked with some date that fell within a period of fifty years after the restoration of Charles the Second; and fixed to the beams of the upper floor was row of cupboards....one or two small tables, together with chairs and benches, gave seats to all the party there assembled ... under the rafters were suspended bunches of herbs for cooking, hams sometimes for export, flitches of bacon, legs of beef, and other articles salted for domestic use...' (8)

That, declared Adam Sedgwick, waxing enthusiastic about the readings from Robinson Crusoe or Pilgrim's Progress, is not drawn 'from my imagination'. It does, however, carry something of a glow in the telling which is accounted for by the fact that he is recalling his childhood.

It remains, to avoid misunderstanding, to give some account of one other present occupied 'house' in the valley. Beck House belies its name in that it never was a dwelling house, but a 'field' house and there are parallel names to be found on the map, for example 'Michael's House', 'Low House' and 'High House'. It was a laithe for storing hay and wintering cattle. The cattle were at one end and the 'mew' at the other end received the hay from the field. We have built into the living area some of the timbers including the 'ridstakes' to which the cattle would be tethered. The settle stones and 'boose' which formed the floor have been covered with cement, or have been set out in the patio outside the main door. The kitchen window is an enlargement of the 'mucking hole', and the small inset in the kitchen wall, is where the farmer would store his cattle medicines, and drenching horn, and anything else he needed. The upstairs window, which looks up the dale, was the 'fork-hole' through which the mew was filled. As we have already indicated it probably dates from the mid eighteenth century.

· · · · ·

1: Wills, Archdeanery of Lonsdale. Lancashire Record Office. Preston. By permission of the County Archivist. WRW L.
2: Loose papers Cumbria Record Office, Kendal, WDFC F.
3: M.E. Garnett : The great rebuilding in Lonsdale. The Transactions of the Historic Society of Lancashire and Cheshire. 1988.
4: Julia Vigour Green : Recollections of Sedbergh School and Town in Early Victorian Times (c 1900). Quoted Sedbergh Historian.
5: Feinnes : Op cit.
6: Wordsworth. Guide to the Lakes (1810). Ed Ernest de Selincourt, 1906, OUP p 123.
7: Marie Hartly and Joan Ingilby : Life and tradition in the Yorkshire Dales. 1968 Dalesman books p 61.
8: Adam Sedgwick's Dent : Memorial by the Trustees of Cowgill Chapel, 1868. 1984 with an introduction by David Boulton, Hobson's Farm, Cowgill, Dent, Cumbria.

PERSECUTION REACHES GRISDALE

The Quaker people were a methodical people. They carefully wrote down everything they did in the local Preparative meetings, the monthly area meetings and the quarterly district meetings. Eventually a report went to London. This was also true of their 'sufferings for truth'. Locally, and nationally, they wrote down what their people suffered, the final account being preserved in 'The Great Book of Sufferings' in London.

Soon after the year 1700 someone, possibly Richard Harrison of Dent, sat down to write :

> 'A Record of some of the Sufferings, of the People of God called Quakers, Belonging to the Monthly Meeting of Sedbergh, in the County of Yorke, in 4 Parts'

His elegant script, and compelling account, make it easy to read. As we have seen in the early years many Quakers in romote dales, such as Grisdale, were connected with the Brigflatts meeting house because their meetings were not yet established, nor yet were their meeting houses built. For that reason we read, in 'Harrison's' account, their story also.

Each of the four parts of the Record goes back to the accession of Charles II when repressive acts had been passed against Quakers and other non-conformists. The exception is the third part which goes back to 1655 to pick up the long-running battle over tithes. Part four is very short.

The story begins with the indictment, in 1663, of more than twenty Quakers in Sedbergh for refusing to attend their parish church. They were taken to prison in York, but eventually released, and in subsequent years suffered distraint of goods for non-payment of fines. In 1675 Friends from Grisdale were indicted, for the same reason, with others at the Quarter Sessions at Weatherby and Pontefract. They were eventually allowed to return home.

In 1681 George Mason, of Dent, John Dent and James Dirkington both of Sedbergh, and Anthony Mason of Grisdale were indicted :

> 'for Twenty pounds per month, for being Absent from their Parish Churches, so called. But the Ground charging and serving those writts was non-payment of Tyth'

The writs were delivered to a tithe farmer who served them, 'one James Moon of Dent, a Bayliff...who went cunningly about serving the said writs'. Here the record becomes quite dramatic and, as James Moon set to work first of all upon a man from Grisdale, I quote that part of the document in full :

A Record, of Some of the Sufferings, of the People
of God called Quakers, Belonging to
the Monthly Meeting of Sedbergh,
in the County of YORKE, in 4 parts,
— viz —

1. Containing an Account, of Some of their
Sufferings for Non-conformity, viz for Absenting
from y National Worshipp, and not Receiving
y Sacrament, so called.

2. An Account, of Some of their Sufferings, for
Meeting = together to Worshipp God, in Spirit & in Truth.

3. An Account, of Some of their Sufferings, For
Denying to pay Tythes, Easter-Reckonings, Steeple-
house = Taxes, & other Such like Demands, w.ch for
Conscience Sake they Refuse to pay.

4. An Account, of Some of their Sufferings, For
Refusing to Swear, or Marrying not according
to y National Form, or for Speaking to Priests, or
others, as moved of y Lord, & for other Testimonies
for y Truth, not brought in under the foregoing heads.

'First he served one upon Anthony Mason and persuaded him to Give appearance to the writt, for if he did so, he knew, he would warrant him, that, the matter would never proceed further, and many more fair and smooth words he used, and pretended kindness as a neighbour. And whereas in the writt was some mention made of the said Antho:Mason being Indebted unto the King and the said Anthony Witton, the sum of Two hundred and Twenty pounds, whereas he did not owe one farthing unto either of them that he knew of, and that statute being made against papists, wch he was not; and therefore ought not to suffer for one. And Reasoning and Consulting in this wise together, believed the said Bayliffe, and the said Anthony Mason and the Bayliffe proffereing him to take his own appearance, without being bound with him or for him, and doe but consent to give his appearance, he might have his liberty forthwith, without being staid or Kept his prisoner being at further charges at that time; Thus did the said Bayliffe overcome that honest man, who had not been acquainted with such exercises, and the Bayliffe laboured to get the said Anthony to give his appearance to the Writt, before that any Friends knew thereof who would have Given Advice, not to have given appearance to the Writt, but rather to have gone to prisson in that Case wch is likely he would have done, if he had been advised first with Friends: But he too much trusted the faire flattering words of the Bayliffe, and so Consented to Give his Appearance, which accordingly was done'.

On the basis of his success with Anthony Mason of Grisdale James Moon next tried the same ploy with John Dent and, succeeding there, he moved on to James Dirkington and George Mason. He succeeded with James Dirkington, but George Mason refused to be persuaded. After that :

' the said Bayliffe served the next writt upon George Mason and kept him prissoner neer three dayes .. and Anthony Fawcett, before named, .. did very much threaten George, but first offered George three wayes to make his choice upon, Viz, pay of for the Tythes he was behind, or Give appearance to that writt, or else Goe to prisson: But if he chused to goe to Prisson, and doe neither thother two wayes, he should be made so, and so greatly to suffer; But all these threats did little move George'.

In the end the document gives us no outcome of the dispute, but goes on to deal with the sufferings the Quakers endured for holding meetings for worship.

It was required that any accusation against them be supported by the testimony of two witnesses, and that those accused must have been heard to pray or to sing, and not just to have been seen sitting in silence. The unsavoury spectacle is presented to us of spies and informers lurking outside Quaker meetings waiting until the Spirit moved someone to testify or sing. After this the spies would rush off and present a complaint to the justices. In 1660 :

> 'Severall of the People of God, Called Quakrs, being peaceably Mett together to waite upon and worshippe the Lord at the House of Thomas Blaikling in Sedbergh, were by the Constable and others apprehended, and several of them Carried before one John Ashton (called a Justice) about 20 miles of but at that time Returned back again. But within a few days after were (for the offence aforesaid (so called) ordered to be brought before him and some other Justices (so called) at Skipton, and there the said Justice, Chiefly to Ensnare Friends, Caused the Oath of Allegiance to be tendered unto them, But Friends for conscience sake toward God, and in obedience to the Comands of Christ. Matt 5, was not free to swear at all'.

This caused them to be committed to prison at York where about 500 Friends were incarcerated, who, after six or seven weeks, were set at liberty by the King's order.

In 1665 the same group of Friends suffered a particularly bad assault at the house of John Blaikling at Drawell, in Sedbergh, when :

> 'Lawrence Hodgson of Dent, who was ensign to the Millitia or Train-band ... behaved himself very rudely, cursing and swearing and threatening that if Friends would not depart and disperse, he and they would kill, and slay and what not: he houlding a pistol Cocked, and also armed with a sword and made himself very furious and terrible but all that did not avail to disperse Friends, nor break the meeting'.

Eventually the worshippers were forced out of the house but refused to follow Hodgson to Sedbergh, so :

> 'in a fury came back the ensign and with his sword drawn, he struck at several Friends, and cut some in the hatt, and some in the clothes and so forced and drave Friends on to Sedbergh town, and would not suffer Jon Blaiklings wife to goe into her house to take a hat for to put on her head'.

Once again the Friends got home in peace. The sufferings of Friends were sometimes aggravated by the attitude of the Justices, and sometimes relieved by them. Later in 1665 a group of Friends from Sedbergh, Dent, Killington and Garsdale were taken before Justice Slinger : 'the said Justice Slinger did much mock, jeer and deride Friends'; but, later, they were 'sett at Liberty by the Kindness of Sir John Otway towards his neighbors and Country men, it being agt Harvest time, wch kindness was well attested of'.

The writer's bitterest criticism was reserved for the informers, often neighbouring farmers, who not only informed against Friends but were allowed to distrain on them when fines were not paid. They also became the men who sold the distrained goods. In general more was taken in distraint than was necessary, and, when sold, no balance was returned to those from whom it had been taken, but simply pocketted by the sellers.

When the persecutors themselves fell on evil days even charitable Friends found it hard not to see in their enemy's misfortune the judgement of God. In particular John Bower and Mark Petty were the object of Friends' disgust for they were :

> 'notorious wicked persons who made themselves as hard-hearted as they could and put the fear and dread of ye Lord farr away from them, and also shamelassness as men, and without love or regard to their friends and neer neighbours, and so fitted themselves for their masters worke, besides giving themselves up to drunkenness and swearing and foreswearing, boasting of their doings and promising great things to bring to pass and got much gain to themselves and their families and to make them Rich thereby'.

The document continues :

> 'Now observe what befell these Informers; The said John Bower was indicted for perjury ... he fled away and got into the King's army ... afterwards he returned but being poor and silly as to his outward man, none medeled with him ... untill he was visited with sickness unto death, in wch time of sickness and weakness The Terrors of Hell seized upon him and he sometimes cryed out that the Devill was about him ready to have him away, and he would have some of his children that were with him to goe out of ye Room that they might not see the Devill carry him away and so terrified those that heard his expressions at some times; and sometimes he said to his daughter Give him some milk to Coole his tongue for he must endure hell fire and hell torments for ever and ever ... he wished that his mother's womb had been his tomb, and in a little time ended his life in this world'.

The passage continues : 'God is Just and will reward the wicked and ungodly with vengeance and torment for ever and ever', and it concludes : 'Blessed be God the hopes of the wicked is often frustrated and the innocent preserved out of the mouths of ravenous wolves and greedy devourers'.

The next mention of Grisdale in the document is of how, in 1683, 'Mabel wife of Richard Harrison, Emma Capstacke, Emma Dawson, Elizabeth Wilkinson all of Dent and Agnes Regnoldson of

Grisdale' were sent by Justice Henry Bouth of Ingleton to the sessions at Pontefract :

> 'which was a great journey for women to undergo, being about a hundred miles back and forwards, and not a man in their company, but that John Mason gave up to accompany and assist them in that exercise, and most of the women had never been 20 miles distant, travelled in all their life'.

After appearing at the sessions they were allowed to return home. Agnes Regnoldson was the sister of Margaret Regnoldson, who was named in March 1679 at the monthly meeting at Hallbank, where arrangements were made for her marriage to John Winn. Agnes, herself, married Edmund Winn of Grisdale on the 2nd of March 1687. After this experience Friends noticed a loop-hole in the law and :

> 'spoke to the said Jno Otway and tould him that the Act of the 22 Car 2 by wch he shewed to have acted; that it did not mention a woman preacher, or teacher, then afterwards he called in his warrant and granted another, in which he left out the fine for a woman speaking, and also the fine for John Hugill who was a poor man'.

It was particularly hard that Friends, already in prison, could be fined if their house was used for a meeting in their absence. Richard Harrison of Dent Town had been in prison in York for five months when on 'ye 16th day of ye Xth mo called December in ye year 1683' a group of his friends worshipped in his house, and Harrison was fined £20 for it. The Quakers complained, but the Justice said : 'that (the) house was a Public noted meeting house constantly once in a month'. Full five pages are filled with the names of those who had distraints made against them for meeting in worship, and the amount of the distraint. The amounts vary from 5/- to £6:13:0. These many seem trivial amounts in terms of today, but we have to set against this the fact that inventories of the time show that a cow was worth about £2. James Guy, John Raw, Bryan Clarke, Willm Goldington and Ann Harrison are described as 'from Garsdale' but as the meetings were not separate at that time some of them could have been from Grisdale.

It is noticable that attempts were made to put Quakers out of business. John Dawson, a smith, had his 'Anvill, Bellows, hammers and other things' taken from him; and Richard Harrison had many things taken out of his shop, which 'almost destroyed him'. One or two people, like Edward Branthwaite and Thomas Harrison, had their fines paid by relatives who were not Quakers.

Section three of the document, like all the others, goes back to 1660 and deals with the refusal to pay tithes. We have already noticed Reynold Winn's struggle against Trinity

College, Cambridge, and the Rector of Sedbergh. The document states :

> 'In the year 1655, These seven persons under mentioned ... were carried before the justices ... distress was made on their goods as followeth :

and among the names we find :

> 'Taken from Thomas Winn of Grisdale, for Tythes, Easter Reckinings for the value of 10s 3d, a mare worth £4:0:0. Note that there was not any of the overplus of any of the said distresses proffered to be Returned to ye owners'.

The date of Thomas Winn's death was 1697, but I have found no will for him, though I have found the will of Edmund Winn his son. What relation he was to Reynold Winn, and his brother John Winn, is impossible to establish, though they lived in the same dale within 20 years of each other.

The year 1655 was still in the Commonwealth period and the account goes on the describe the abuses heaped on Friends who attempted to preach at the time:

> 'stoning, clodding, and other abuses, besides scoffing, mocking, Railing, and the like, all which Friends endured with great patience'.

Ten years later we read :

> 'In the year 1665 Thomas Middleton of Dent, who was then become Farmer of the Tythes of Sedbergh, Dent, Garsdale and Grisedale' distrained on ten people among whom he 'Gott from Thomas Winn of Grisedale in sheepe, and otherwise, about the value of three pounds ten shillings'.

In 1668 :

> 'Thomas Winn of Grisdale, for denying to pay a small sum in Lieu if Tythes, had taken from him by the sd Richard Trotter & Anthony Fawcett, Tyth Farmers, four ewes, worth thirty shillings. In the same year the said Thomas Winn, for denying to pay an Assess of eleven shillings , towards the rebuilding of the Steeple house, or Bell house, in Garsdale, had a cow taken from him by John Norton & Edward Dent called wardens, & George Holland a Constable, worth forty shillings & no overplus returned'.

The report added :

> 'It is not many years since the said Thomas Middleton his own selfe denyed the payment of Tythes; but not for Conscience sake; but as not being due, by reason of some special Act of Abba free, or upon such Acts as he had to,

and did, declare; and many persons within Dent, and there
were away, was of the same opinion with him, and Joined
with him, in defence of the same agst those of the College
wch Claimed and comensed suit agst them; And the said
Thomas Middleton believed they had gained the cause agst
the Collegians, but that he blamed some of Dent for
Conveying, or wronging of some writings wch specially
concerned the same, to their great disadvantage in the
case'.

The list of distraints continued from year to year. In 1679 :

'Edmund Winn, of Grisdale, for a small matter, prtended
due for Tyths had taken from him, by the same psons, and
for the same Tyth Farms a beast worth...' (no price
given).

Neighbours must often have felt that the Quakers were
suffering unjustly for in the very early 1700's the tithe
farmers for Grisdale gathered up several cattle in order to
sell them, except :

'that, friends tould them they would not allow off, so
they turned them out into the street or high way, and this
so grieved the said Tythmen that now when they ran to
prsecute friends of Grisdale, They claimed a Tyth for 3
years and divided it into two actions and got costs
granted for either action'.

There was obviously a certain sympathy for the Quakers, and,
indeed, the document goes further and suggests that the Rector
of Sedbergh, on whose behalf the tithe farmers were acting,
felt that they overstepped the mark. In 1681 :

'The said Francis Lund and Thomas Salkelt were Continued
in prisson till after the death of both the priest and
proctor aforesaid, and then sett at Liberty by the free
Consent of the priests widdow. Within the time of
imprisonment Thomas Salkelt wife died and Lost 2 children;
They were Released in the 5th mo 1681. The aforesaid
Priest often was sorry and repented that he had gott the
said Proctor Nuton on work upon that account'.

In 1693 Anthony Fawcett (who had been a tithe farmer for more
that 25 years) was :

'taken with a palsie so that he was Lame on one side, and
not able to go or ride alone without somebody to help him,
so that he was hindered of executing his will & mind. But
that affliction on his body did not prevail in him to work
him into repentance & amendment for what he had done
against the innocent and faithful people of God above
mentioned, altho he was vissitted by some friends when he
was under his deep affliction in order to see if theii

would find any rebuting or repentance or sorrow, but there was no such thing found with him, but great hardness of heart remaining in him, & he stood by what he had done, nevertheless Ye people of God do send help to his suffering people & shew him mercy & kindness'.

It is sad to read that two years later Anthony Fawcett sued James Harker of Grisdale before the Bishop's Court at York and had him committed to prison in York Castle. The report added :

'He was hardened in heart, without pitty even towards good & honest men as was James Harker, he Leaving a wife & many Children, for the Trueth & good Conscience sake'. and :

'About in ye 3rd mo, called May, An 1696, dyed the said Antho Faw[cett] without heaving Repentance for what he had done agt Friends & left James Harker in prisson'.

The last, pages of the document record that at the Quarter Sessions held at Skipton on July 15th 1701 :

'the new erected house at Lea Yate in Dent belonging to Thomas Mason etc be Recorded as a place for Religious worship pursuant to the late Act of Parliament intitled an Act for exempting His Majts protestant subjects dissenting from the Church of England from the penalties of sundry laws'.

The same page recorded the licensing of the Garsdale meeting house, and the following page recorded that 'in the third year of the reign of our sovereign Lord and Lady King William and Queen Mary' the houses of Edmund Winn and Mich. Dawson were licenced for public worship. These both lived in Grisdale where, five years later, the meeting house was to be built. There is no mention of where in Grisdale they lived but there is some reason to think the Winns were at Scale, and the land for the meeting house which was built five years later was bought from Eleanor Dawson of Round Ing. Perhaps the first Quaker meetings were held at Scale and Round Ing; among the most remote houses in the dale.

It might be thought, from such an entry as the one above, that the sufferings were over. It was not so, for the Quakers still refused to pay tithes and book after book in the County Record Office, going on well into the next century, tells of the continued distraints.

. . . . .

The source for this chapter is 'A Record of some of the Sufferings of the People of God called Quakers, belonging to the Monthly Meeting of Sedbergh, in the County of Yorks, in 4 Parts' : Cumbria Record Office, Kendal : WDFC F.

A Register, of the
Birthes,
Marriages,
&
Burialls;

of the People of God,

called Quakers,
of
Garsdale & Grisdale
in the County of Yorke;
~ ~ ~ ~
With an Account of Some of their
Sufferinge for the Trueth, /

BURIED AT SCALE

Any walker who has reached the two derelict houses of East and West Scale may imagine that he knows the meaning of the word 'remote', but it requires a considerable effort of imagination to conceive how really cut off these houses were in previous centuries. We can now travel on a good motor road as far as East House and, if we can find a convenient place to leave our car, we can follow the river bank until, in less than half an hour, we cross the bridge at Scale. If we look to the right at that point we shall see a small tree-enclosed field by the river side behind East Scale. No stone marks the spot, but this is the Quaker burial ground.

Standing there in the silence we may try to imagine what it must have cost to bring bodies there for burial from the different parts of the Grisdale valley when only tracks existed. We shall need an even greater act of imagination to imagine what it must have cost in human labour to carry a loved one down for burial at Garsdale church yard six or seven miles away in the sixteenth and seventeenth centuries before the opening of the Scale burial ground, or the existence of the turnpikes. Those who, like Edmund Winn in 1587, made their wills and required from their executors and supervisers that their bodies be buried in Garsdale church yard were laying a considerable obligation on them. It is no wonder that the Grisdale Quakers, as the inner light dawned and the ties with the established Church were severed, hid themselves behind the barrier of half a mile of moorland in the days of persecution and began to bury their dead in land of their own.

According to a recently discovered tithe map of Grisdale the road we know did not exist in 1841, in its present form. It may have been made as a result of the destruction of the 'old' road and bridges by the flood of 1889, and coincides with the building of the chapel in that year. What road, or cart track, there was before that crossed Bow Bridge below Beck House, and re-crossed the river twice before it came to Reacher. It crossed to the north side of the river once more near the Quaker meeting house site from which it made its way to 'Near' and 'Far' Scale. At these crossing points there may have been, at one time, bridges which were washed away in the 1889 flood. Between Beck House and Reacher a track went north to Moor Rigg, East House and Kirby Stephen. This was joined by another track above Round Ing which came from Ravenstonedale and went past Flust and East House to Lunds, Hawes and Kirby Stephen.

Further down the valley what roads there were in the early days must have been like the green lanes, or drover's roads, which can still be seen threading their way, now in seeming aimlessness, on the middle or upper reaches of the fells. The

A684 did not exist and the turnpikes which preceded it are of
relatively late date in our story. It was on the 12th of
January 1792 that Samuel Lund of 'Rantree' set his mark and
seal to his will in which he left 'the money that I s(p)ent on
the Turnpike securities' (30 years before) to his grandson,
Samuel, as well as the 'freehold called and commonly known as
Cock and Gomgutter situate in Garsdale'. This land may have
bordered the new road.

The turnpike was really the tollgate set up on the road at
which those who built the road collected tolls for the passage
of goods along these much improved highways which superseded
the drover's roads. Along the drover's roads wool and stockings
had gone out of Grisdale on pack horses for centuries. Perhaps
the best way to imagine what a turnpike road was like is to
look with imagination at the piece of road that runs between
the two signposts marked 'Grisdale' on the A684. That narrow
'Grisdale old road,' coming from the direction of Sedbergh,
winds up past Grouse Hall before it passes the junction to the
Grisdale valley. It then goes on to join the A684 towards Hawes
Junction and the Moorcock. It is part of the greatly improved
turnpike road of 1761 which linked Sedbergh with Askrigg. It is
named 'old road' in contrast to the A684 in the valley bottom
which is the 1825 diversion. The 1761 road was joined in 1765,
at Hawes Junction, where the Moorcock was built about 1825, by
another turnpike which went down Mallerstang to Kirby Stephen.
So 'Hawes Junction' was so named 80 years before the coming of
the railway.

In our cars today we may not think much of Grisdale old road
with its narrow twists and passing places, but it is of the
dimensions of a turnpike road : about 18 feet wide between the
walls or trenches on either side and with a hard surface about
12 feet wide. When built this would be gravelled and take
carriages and horse traffic. Before those days people walked
or, if they could afford it, went on horseback. Edmund Winn,
who made his will in 1587, left his 'horse, saddle and bridle
with other riding gear' to his younger son, Leonard. The wills
of Nicholas Winn (1623) and Robert Winn (1632) make a similar
provision, and several other wills mention horses. Poorer
people, and the women, walked whether it was to Sedbergh for
the monthly meeting, or Kendal for the quarterly meeting or
even to Pontefract if they were summoned to the assize. We may
imagine, in a time without street lighting, that they would
travel by day or, if forced to go by night, would choose the
nights of the full moon.

In the year 1694, just after the establishment of Quaker
meetings first at Garsdale, and then at Grisdale, someone began
to look back to the early days and record the burials at Scale
from 1679, the births in the valley from from 1651 and the
marriages from 1689. He wrote in a bold clear hand and called
it :

BURIED AT SCALE

A Register, of the
Birthes,
Marriages,
Burialls;
of the People of God,
called Quakers,
of Garsdale, & Grisdale
in the County of Yorke;
....
With an Account of some of their
Sufferings for the Trueth.

After that first writer ceased his labours five or six other
hands in each category carried on the story until 1835. It is
possible that, especially in the latter years, every birth,
marriage or burial is not recorded. The writers seem to have
run out of steam; for we have a request to the grave digger,
John Blades, for a burial in 1843 which is not included, and
there may be others. (1)

There are about a hundred burials recorded in the Scale
burial ground, and there must be more which are not in the
record. In the Garsdale burial ground are about 90 burials.
This burial ground lies behind a small gate on the left hand
side of the road as you go down the Garsdale valley a few
hundred yards before you come to Garsdale Street.

What can we learn about these silent people who lived in so
quiet a place and who are buried beside the silent stream?

I must write with caution because, like the dalesman of
today, they were reticent and, even in their dying
declarations, they said so little about themselves. It is only
by reading between the lines that we gain some idea of what
sort of people they were.

'Dales hospitality' is proverbial and this must account for
the 1704 report from the minutes of the Kendal quarterly
meeting about hospitality at funerals :

> 'It advises that no Friends hereafter take any thing to
> carry away with them, onley eat and drink what may be
> necessary for ye time. And where any friends give any
> victuals to persons invited that they give no more bread
> drink etc...' presumably than was necessary. (2)

It was the custom of the more ostentatious people of the world
to 'feast their neighbours' on such occasions. It was the
eighteenth century equivalent of being 'buried with ham'. The
Kendal meeting laid it down that if bread and cheese and drinks
were to be given :

> 'let it be in a modest plain way without what is comon and
> costomary superfluity among other people and not above one

THE SILENT STREAM

Frontage of East Scale

K.E.Kohn.

EAST SCALE and SCALE BRIDGE

Bridge by East Scale

loaf at most to a person, and in some places halfe may be sufficient'.

It was recognised, however, that in country places some refreshment was necessary for people had come a long way.

When we turn to the wills that have survived we find that each one begins with the 'legacy' of the soul of the testator to God, with the devout hope of salvation by the merits of Jesus Christ, and the desire that arrangements might be made for decent burial. The concern is not just for suitable disposal but a wish that the testator might be 'honestly brought forth', that is that his debts might be paid off by the day of his funeral. (3)

From that point the wills of the men are concerned mainly with the correct disposal of their lands and tenements and concern for the future provision of their widows, and what children they had.

The wills left by the women, in the pre-Quaker period, are much more interesting. They have a proper female interest in their clothing which they dispose of to others who might appreciate it. Fashion was not, in those days, the tyranny it is today and sober people felt no shame in the inheritance of a splendid garment. In 1648 Dorothy Winn left her bible to Ann Bland, and her 'best redd petticoate' to her sister, Elizabeth. In the same way her 'best hatt', her 'best ruffed band', a 'white happin', 'yarne and stockings', 'a petticote with a lethern bodice', 'my best white coate', 'my double happin' and a 'browne carsey coate' went to the wives and daughters of friends, and her 'greatest pan but one' to Dorothy Hobson. A ruffed band would be a gophered neck band, a happin was a coverlet or quilt and 'Carsey' was, even then, an obsolete word for 'Kersey', a ribbed, rough worsted, sometimes called Kendal worsted. In 1650 Grace Winn, wife of Robert Winn who died in 1632, disposed of 'a redd petticote, a Gowne, a Couerlitt, one pare of Furred gloves, one Hatt' as well as giving twelve pence to every child for whom she had been God-mother.

There is the occasional note of patriarchal dominance. Thomas Winn said in 1777 : 'my daughter May Winn shall have the chist that she calls hers'; and Thomas Winn of Reacher said in 1775 'it is also my will that the money Bequeathed to my wife in John Airey's Last Will be att her own Disposal'. No doubt the two ladies imagined those things were their own in any case.

There is also to be found an occasional note of family concern. Michael Dawson of Moor Rigg, who died in 1730, left his land in trust for his grand-daughters, Elizabeth and Mary Adamthwaite, who were minors. He left his son-in-law, William, two pounds ten shillings a year for each of the girls until they became 21 years of age. But he added :

'if my trustees observe, know, or have notice of any hard
usage or ill-treatment of my said grand-daughters ... and
if he do not find them Meat, Drink, Apparell, Washing,
Lodging, Education and Learning sufficient and suitable to
their state, degree and condition ...' the money was to be
withdrawn.

Do we detect a hint of a family dispute, or was it just a dying
grand-father's anxiety?

It is a pity that in wills before the eighteenth century the
testator usually said that he was 'of Grisdale', and only later
do we hear of 'Scale', 'Flust', 'Aldershaw' and other farms.
The inventories which accompany the wills give us some idea of
what these house might contain. It is not surprising that a
common term for a man's house was his 'firehouse' when we read
of cauldrons, griddles, 'racans' (a chain or vertical bar on
which pots were suspended over a fire), pans, spits, kettles,
ratchets and tongs, a frying pan, gridirons, a brandreth (a
three legged iron tripod for use on a hearth), a cocklepan (a
shallow dish for use on the fire), and a cresset (an iron fire
basket for setting a pot on the fire). To these were added
pewter, wooden vessels (treen), brass vessels, sheets,
blankets, bedstocks, arks (chests for the storage of oatmeal),
and pewter doublers, that is a pewter plate so made that you
could turn it upside down. In this way a second 'course' could
be eaten off the same plate. There were chairs and stools,
chists, cushions, a cheese press, a dish-bench, spinning
wheel, an hour glass, and cards for carding wool. Only when we
approach the 1800's do we read of 'a clock'.

Some idea of the daily diet of the people of the dale may be
gleaned from the inventories. They list (oat) meal, beef,
butter, cheese, bacon and malt. Little else appears.

From the same source we may get some idea of the farming
equipment which was in use, though this is often described as
'husbandry gear'. However, in the will of Leonard Winn, who
died in 1631, we read of :

'a stone hamer, thre iran weydges, a Sharkle, two true
boutes, a pare of Tormederoes, two flaying spades, another
spaide, a harke, a hockte spade, two womels, two axes, six
haire Ropes, thre pare of tracses, a warrow, a garth
barhum and hames, a shepe hecke, two stolles, a Iron forke
and anewdore'.

To translate : a barum is a collar for a working horse, a hecke
is a rack for holding hay in a field. Womel is an obsolete word
for a wimble, that is a gimlet or auger; while 'hockte' means
hooked. Warrow is a harrow, and hames are iron parts of a horse
collar. 'Tormederoes' have eluded me, and everyone else.

In the will of Robert Winn, who died in 1639 near Sedbergh, there is mention of a 'coulewock, a gavel and a lister'. These are a coulter, an instument for gathering corn into a sheaf, and a double-moulded plough which threw up ridges and buried the seed at the same time. More than one will in the pre-Quaker period mentions : 'his sword'.

There are, also, two persistent strains which run through the Quaker wills of the Winn family beginning in the 1670's. One is that they lived at Scale, at least for some part of the time, and the other is that they were 'stockiners' or 'hosiers'. In many wills quantities of wool are mentioned and Reynold Winn in 1677 left wool worth £6, almost equal to the total value of the estates of other men. It must be said, also, that the wills of the Dawson and Dent families, which I have read, make many references to wool. Indeed, there is scarcely an inventory of any length which does not mention 'wooll and stockings'.

In 1734 Robert Rawe died at one of the Scale houses, and was described as a 'carrier'. Among his effects were :

Eight stone and a half of skin wool	£4: 10: 0
Twelve dozen of spotted socks	£1: 4: 0
A clock, a weather glass and a map	£1: 12: 6

He also owned 'six pack saddles, wantows and girths belonging to the same'. 'Wantow' was an obsolete form of 'wanty', which was itself an obsolete word to describe a rope used to fasten the pack on to the saddle of a pack horse. No doubt the clock, weather glass and map were essential to such a travelling man.

To our eyes Scale is remote but it could have been on a pack horse route on the 'road' that runs across the top of the valley from Ravenstonedale, past Flust and East House to Lunds, Mallerstang and Kirby Stephen. Robert Rawe, as a pack horse master, could have lived in a strategic place. Perhaps Reynold Winn, seventy years earlier, had been a wholesaler for all the many knitters of the dale. As we have seen he was a man who was involved in many things and the number of times his name appears on wills as a witness, or 'pricer', with the names of John Close, Michael Dawson, James Wilson and Arthur Regnoldson, testifies to the leading part he took in the dale's affairs, and those of the Quaker brotherhood.

In the early 1500's 'netherstocks' had been made from cross-cut worsted and sewn on to breeches, or cross-gartered (after the fashion of Malvolio) if they were not sewn. Soon after this they began to be knitted in the round using four needles, two held in the hand and the others kept in place in hand-carved needle holders which were thrust into the belt or skirt top. It is still possible to find these today in antique shops. Wherever wool was available everybody knitted. 'The terrible knitters of Dent' have quite a reputation. Men, women and children, as well as labourers and soldiers all needed stockings if they worked outside and thousands of people in the dales knitted throughout the centuries to supply them.

We do not know who gave the land to the Quakers for the burial ground at Scale. It is possible it was Reynold Winn. The fact that it was 'given' was understood, but it was never conveyed so it has passed on with the farm to successive owners. When Reynold Winn died he, as a Quaker, gave no instructions for his body to be buried in Garsdale church yard, but he did leave £20 to provide an income for a schoolmaster in Grisdale. This is both testimony to the number of children who needed to be taught and the determination of the Quakers to keep their children separate from the teachings of the 'steeple-houses'. A few years later Christopher Winn also began a school in Brigflatts, which he continued until 1710. The will of John Close, Junior, who died in 1715, included a gift of £5 towards the schooling of children in Grisdale.

Reynold Winn in his will mentioned no children of his own but left considerable sums to the children of John, his brother. I have wondered if Anthony Winn, who died before Reynold Winn in 1675, could have been Reynold Winn's son? He left assets of only £2:6:8, and debts of £4:13:7, plus an axe, a spade, a fork, a bed and little else. He lived in a house which was not inventoried. Perhaps he might have expected to inherit from Reynold Winn who was a 'pricer' in his will. Certainly we imagine that the Quaker care for the poor saw to it that Anthony Winn's wife, Jane, did not lack for anything.

Though Abraham Dent, who died in 1679, is the first recorded burial at Scale, it is possible that Reynold Winn and his wife are buried there, especially if, as I have imagined, he gave the land for the purpose. Certainly his brother, John, was buried there in 1683, as was John's daughter, Ruth, in 1716. Abraham Dent left Moor Rigg to his son, John, with instructions that he should pay 'twenty pounds of current English money to every child of mine that shall be living an equal portion'. It is to be hoped that his intention was that the twenty pounds should be shared, for he left liquid assets of £9:7:9 and debts of £14:13:0.

Reynold Winn left half of his estate to John Close Senior, but there is no hint as to what the relationship might have been which caused him to do so. Was there a family tie, or was it that they were both very much involved in the Quaker movement? John Close, Junior, left a will which he made in 1715 being :

    'for a journey and not knowing when my Return may be, nor ye time of my departure out of ys Life'.

He was a notable Quaker travelling minister and the records of the Brigflatts monthly meeting tell us that in 1714 he was given a certificate to visit Friends 'in Bishoprick', which is almost certainly Durham. In 1715 he was given a certificate to visit Friends and preach in 'Cheshire and places adjacent some parts of Wales'. In the tenth month of the same year :

> 'John Close and Jn Hugginson signified to this meeting that hey had Drawings upon their Spirit to Visit Friends in Cumberland and some places Adjacent'.

The certificate was give and they went on their journey. Two months later :

> 'John Hugginson returned the Certificate which he and John Close had along with them into Cumberland and gave accot [account] that when they had mostly Performed the service before them (wch was to Satisfaction) John Close was taken ill of the Small Pox, and Died on the 27th of the 11th month at the House of Robt Becbey of Allonby in Cumberland, and was decently Buryed in Friends Burying Ground on the 29th of the same'. (4)

For some reason his will was not proved until 1734 and in it he mentioned with affection his father and mother. Here is the relevant quotation with other matters in the will:

> 'I give to my Honouyred Father and Mother ye House at Low flust in wch they now dwell, & ye fold or parrock in wch the House standeth, Excepting ye little house in ye low end of it'

They were to pay to Thomas Close, his brother and executor, 'a Reasonable sum of money for it, not Exceeding one pound tenn shillings a yeare'. The will continued :

> 'I give to my well-beloved friend Margaret Adamthwaite of Ravenstonedale five pounds ... my Bible and Best Handkerchief'.

The gift seems so warmly bestowed that we wonder if there was a special relationship between them, especially as John Close would have been of marriagable age. His brother, Thomas, married Margaret Rogerson in 1717. Other gifts follow :

> 'five pounds towards maintaining a school in Grysdale ... two pounds to be divided among ye poor people of Garsdale and Grysdale ... I give to my maidservant Elisabeth Hugginson one pound'.

So it ended and Michael Dawson and William Adamthwaite solemnly affirmed his signature, the latter, perhaps, hoping as he did so, to be his father-in-law one day.

The foregoing would imply that Reynold Winn's friend, to whom he gave half his land was John Close Senior. Margaret, Mabel and Mary Close figure in the early Grisdale Quaker records. The only recorded Close burial at Scale is that of Sarah, the wife of Thomas Close in 1714, and we have seen that he married again in 1717. If the three 'M's' were his sisters they could well have married and also be buried at Scale among the many with the same Christian names. Mabel certainly married Robert Rogerson in 1724, but there is no record of her burial.

In 1708 Thomas Clemmy was buried at Scale, where his son, also Thomas, had been buried two years before. Mary and Agnes Clemmy were representatives to the monthly meeting at Brigflatts on a number of occasions. Elizabeth, the wife of Thomas Clemmy Senior was buried at Scale in 1716, and Agnes in 1744. Thomas Clemmy died intestate and his inventory was priced by John Close. His goods were worth £48:15:0. His debts were £46.

Eleanor, the wife of Richard Dawson of Round Ing, signed the conveyance of the ground for the meeting house at Stubstacks in 1709 and was buried at Scale by the end of the same year. It would be wasted labour to try to sort out one Michael Dawson from another for two Michael Dawsons had witnessed the will of Reynold Winn in 1677. One Michael Dawson died intestate in 1698 worth £306, and another Michael Dawson signed the conveyance for the meeting house site in 1709. Two Michael Dawsons were buried at Scale in the period, one in 1713 and one in 1730/1. These were not the first, or the last, Michael Dawsons, for another Michael Dawson of Grisdale had made his will in 1652 owning lands at Aldershaw. So the name went on, and I know of at least one Michael Dawson in the Sedbergh area today.

Thomas Winn, who was born in 1687, the son of Edmund and Agnes Winn, was buried at Scale in 1734. His mother had died in 1701 having lived for 16 weeks after the birth of a daughter, Deborah. The register of burials added a note :

'Agnas the wife of Edmond Winn was buried the 26th day of the third month 1701. She lived 16 weeks after she had a child and was very weak at the time as to outward body but exceedingly opn harted unto god whereby she retined in that time great streingth from god to shew forth his prais and often exhorted hir family to feare god with large praises thereupon and she gave hir family much proof always, and the day she died she had a dasier [desire] to God hir children al that she might tak hir live [leave] of them desiered of god to bless them al'

No mention is made of the death of Ann, Thomas's wife, but two of their children, both called Elizabeth were buried at Scale; one in July 1706 and the other in June 1707. They were obviously both infants. Thomas lived at Scale and left the farm to his brother Joseph, and five pounds a year to Sarah Raw, his sister, as well as other cash legacies to members of the Winn family.

Robert Raw of Mousesike, making his will in 1736, left his money on trust for his children and his second wife, adding the proviso that she was to receive the balance of his estate but :

'if she shall ather marey or miscarey then it is my will and minde tht they shall pay hir five shilings and no more for ever'.

Several of the wills I have quoted imply a level of comfort for some inhabitants of the dale, for sums of one, three and six hundred pounds are found in them. These must translate into considerable sums in today's money. Most people seem to have died worth about £20 or so, but some much less. Anthony Clemmy died in 1728 worth £7:9:0 leaving a hammer, a washtrough, some iron and odd small things. Robert Aykrigg died ten years later leaving only his clothes and what was in his purse : £10:15:0. Elenor Dent, who died in 1741, left £1:8:6 and a note in the hand of Thomas Winn for £27. It is when we compare such sums with the amount given, for example, for 'a tenfold collection' for the repair of the meeting house, that we have some measure of Quaker generosity.

When we compare the birth and burial records it is obvious that several families lost children in their earlier years, or in their 'teens'. The repeat in a family of the name of a child some years after the death of the namesake indicates a wish to remember, and in a sense recover, a well-beloved child who died in infancy. The lives of small children were fragile and there is evidence, in earlier centuries, of an unwillingness to invest too much love in them until it was certain they would survive.

In 1740 Thomas Winn of Reacher and Howshawhead was buried at Scale. His wife, who may be the Ann Winn who died in 1713, was a member of the Harker family, perhaps related to Adam and Emma Harker of Low Scale, Garsdale.

In 1777 a further Thomas Winn of Reacher 'an ancient and valuable Publick friend' was buried at Scale. He gave Howshawhead to his daughter, Elizabeth, with 'my clock and the dresser that stands beside it', and to his son, Edmund, 'all the rest of my houses (excepting the house in which I now dwell)'. This was to remain with his wife, Esther, who was to receive £8 a year from his son who also inherited the balance of the goods. Other cash legacies completed the picture.

That Edmund Winn made his will on January 1st 1792. He lived at Feafow which he owned with Reacher, Stubstacks and Flust. He was buried at Scale, aged 61, on March 25th 1792. He divided his land between his two sons, Thomas and William, and gave legacies to his four daughters. He also mentioned a cousin at Raygill in Garsdale, and from this point the strength of the Winn family seems to have moved into Garsdale.

To _James Blades_ Grave-Maker.

The _Third_ Day of the _First_ Day, in Friends⸺

MAKE a Grave on or before next _Eight_ Month, 184_3_

Burial-Ground at or near _Scail in Grisdale_

in the _County_ of _York_

and therein lay the body of _Elizabeth Abriag_

of _Aldershaw_ in the

County of York

aged about _seventy one years_ who died the

Eight Month, One Thousand Eight Hundred and

Forty three

John Williamson

The Body above-mentioned was buried the _Sixth_

Day of the _Eight_ Month, 184_3_

Witness _____ Grave-Maker.

For _Elizabeth Abriag_

of _Aldershaw in Grisdale_

who died the _7_ day of the

Eight month 1843

Delivered to _James Blades_

the _6_ of the 8 mo. 1843

Grave to be made at

Scail in Grisdale

on or before the _Sixth_ day of

the _Eight_ month 1843

SHE WAS POSSIBLY THE DAUGHTER OF THE MAN WHO BUILT ALDERSHAW

It would be wrong to give the impression that Grisdale was totally Quaker. The burial register for the Garsdale parish church contains names which 'belong' to the Quaker families of the dale :

'Margarett Mason of High Scale was buried the fourth day of September Ano Dmi 1696'.

'Margrett wife of Robert Aykrigg of Grisedale was buried the eleventh of October Ano Dmi 1696'

'Michael Dawson of Grisedale buried ye fourth day of January 1698'

Several Raw's were buried in the churchyard between 1724 and 1768.

'John Close late of Grisedale buried Aug. 14th 1746'.

To these deaths may be added marriages and baptisms of members of the same families. Many of the entries in the mid 1700's were in the bold handwriting of the Rev. William Todhunter, Curate. (5)

On October 31st 1797 Philip Thompson signed his will which was proved on December 6th. He was 52 years of age and lived at 'East Houses'. He left eight children, several of them under the age of 21. His brother was John Thompson of Mousesyke. Philip was not buried at Scale but in the Church grave yard at Garsdale. We have already noticed the beginning of a movement away from the Quakers at this time, though one of his executors, Hodgson, 'being a Quaker did solemnly affirm'. Three of his sons aged 28, 25 and 24, on the death of their father, were baptised on the same day at Garsdale parish church. It is possible they had not been baptised because the family had been Quaker, and the Quakers have no sacraments. Were they 'returning to the fold', and re-joining others in the valley? Or, were they attempting to avoid some of the disadvantages the Quakers suffered? A cutting from THE CHRONICLE for Saturday, May 13th 1876, recorded the refusal to bury a Helmsley Quaker 'in God's acre' because he was unbaptised :

> 'he must be buried like a dog ... but a hedge separated the consecrated from the unconsecrated ground. On each side of the hedge, we may assume, the Almighty has jurisdiction ... they buried the Quaker under the hedge in the new burial ground ... while a Primitive Methodist minister impressively read the burial service, with a cart for his pulpit, over the remains from the other side of the hedge'. (6)

I have concentrated in this chapter on the Scale burial ground which is a silent, but tangible, reminder of past days. There is also a record of marriages and a considerable number of births. The whole gives a sense of a caring, integrated, but not uniform, community. The Quaker people of Grisdale looked after each other. They 'mourned with those who mourned, and rejoiced with those who rejoiced', and they cared for their children.

By contrast I found a sad little note in the Garsdale parish registers :

> 'Mary, daughter of one Agnes a stranger, who would not discover her own name or the father's or whence she came, lodged with Rowland Harper of Rackenthwaite, was baptised the eighth of January 1708'. (7)

. . . . .

1: A Register of the Births, Marriages & Burialls; of the People of God, called Quakers, of Garsdale & Grisdale, in the County of Yorke; With an Account of some of their Sufferings for the Trueth. Public Record Office, London. RG6 1197.

2: Kendal Quarterly meeting minutes : Cumbria Record Office, Kendal. WDFC F.

3: All the wills quoted in this chapter are in the Lancashire Record Office, Preston. They belong to the Archdeanery of Lonsdale, and are quoted by permission from the County Archivist. Ref: WRW L.

4: Brigflatts monthly minutes : CRO, Kendal, WDFC F.

5: A Register Book of Weddings, Christenings, & Burials within the Chappelry of Garsdale begun Ano Dni 1693. CRO Preston. WDFC F

6: From loose papers in the Brigflatts Meeting House.

7: Op cit under 5.

LIST OF BURIALS AT SCALE BY YEARS.

The dates in [ ] are the dates (Quaker style) in the Garsdale/Grisdale list from the Public Record Office. The names in ( ) are names of those 'not in unity', and some recorded in other sources. In each case the date given is the date of DEATH. Burial often took place the next day, or within 48 hours.

1679 : Abraham Dent [7:12:1679]
1680 : Elizabeth wife of Thomas Winn [11:3:1680]
1682 : Robert Dent [29:7:1682]: Richard Dawson [9:10:1682]
1683 : John Winn [8:10:1683]
1686 : Agnes wife of Edmund Winn [27:8:1686] NB see 1701.
      Were there 2 families, or is this his first wife?
1687 : Agnes, wife of George Mason [19:1:1687]
1690 : (Michael Dawson, not found in list)
1691 : (Robert Dawson and his wife of East House, not in list)
1696 : (Thomas Winn & Michael Dawson and his wife of East Ho)
      Quakers, but not in list
1698/9 : Elizabeth Marson (MASON) wife of Christopher Mason
            [28:12:1698/9]
1700 : (William Lambert and his wife Mellory (nee Mason) and
      Robert and Margaret Akrigg)
1701 : (Deborah, [5:6;1701] daughter of Edmund and Agnes Winn.
      Agnes Winn who lived 16 weeks after the birth of
      this child, Deborah [26:3:1701].
1702 : (Jane Winn, of Moor Rigg). Mary Winn d of John and
      Margaret Winn [27:10:1702].
      Robart Wilson, s. of Richard, [11:8:1702]
      Isabell Wilson d of Richard [14:10:1702]
      George Marson (Mason) and his daughter Mabell.
1703 : John, son of John Winn and Margaret his wife
      [23:11:1703]. (George Mason and his wife of White
      Wall Head).
1706 : Margaret, wife of Thomas Metcalf [3:3:1706]
      Elizabeth, daughter of Thomas and Ann Winn [28:5:1706].
      Thomas, son of Thomas and Elizabeth Clemmy [7:11:1706]
      Richard Wilson of Garsdale [2:7:1706]
1707 : Ann, daughter of Thomas and Ann Winn [7:4:1707]
1708 : Thomas Clemmy [16:11:1708].
1709 : Elenor, wife of Richard Dawson [8:12;1709]. She sold the
      land for the meeting house.
1710 : Katharn Wilson [24:3:1710].
      (Mary, wife of John Winn, not in list)
1711 : Elizabeth, wife of James Harker, of Garsdale [4:3:1711]
      John Winn, (his wife is Margaret, and son, Thomas)
      [27:9:1711]
1712 : Stephen Dent , [3:1:1712/3] Elizabeth, daughter of
      Samuel Winn [15:5:1712].
1713 : Agnes, wife of Thomas Winn Jnr [19:8:1713]
      Ann Winn, wife of Thomas Winn Snr [18:3:1713]
      Michael, son of Michael Dawson [28:5:1713]
1714 : Sarah Close (nee Dawson) wife of Thomas Close,[3:7:1714]

1715 : Mary, daughter of William Lambert (of White Wall),
       [27:3:1715] Elizabeth Roginson [29:10:1715].
       (John Close [29:11:1715] He was the son of the man
       to whom Reynold Winn gave half his land. He was buried
       at Allonby, but included in the Scale record).
1716 : John Dawson, son of Michael Dawson [4:6:1716]
       Elizabeth Clemmy [13:4:1716]
       Ruth Winn d of John Winn [10:1:1716]
       (Kathleen Wilson widow of Richard Wilson)
1719 : Margret Adamwhayte (nee Dawson) wife of William A.
       [17:10:1719].
1721 : Elizabeth Metcalfe, [28:3:1721]
       Margaret Parker [8:10:1721]
1728 : Arthur Clemmy, (of High Flust, and Cadshaw Bank),
       [7:3:1728]
1729 : Catrain Akridge, wife of Robert Akridge, [25:1:1729]
       Edmund Winn [8:1:1729/30]
1730 : Samuel Winn [6:9:1730], Michael Dawson [5:11:1730/1]
1733 : Margaret Winn, [11:2:1733]
1734 : Thomas Winn [23:3:1734], James Lambert, (father of
       William Lambert) [10:5:1734], Robert Raw [28:2:1734]
       John s of Michael and Elizabeth Akridge [23:1:1734/5]
       Elizabeth [20:12] and Isabella [23:12] Dent. Two
       sisters within 3 days.
1735 : John, s of Michael & Elizabeth Akridge [23:1:1735].
1737 : Jain Dawson, of 'Gasdale' [22:5:1737]
1738 : Robert Akridge [5:2:1738], William Hodgson [18:4:1738]
1739 : Mary Hodgson, [26:5:1739]
1740 : Mabel Lambert [17:3:1740], Thomas Winn [22:9:1740]
1741 : Mary Alderson, [26:12;1741], Elenor Dent [29:4:1741].
1742 : Melory Lambert [16:3:1742], William Alderson [11:6:1742]
1743 : John Hodgson, [31:3:1743], (Mary, d of Edmund Winn)
1744 : Agnes Clemmy, wife of Arthur C, (nee Winn), [6:12:1744]
1746 : William Hodgson [10:5:1746]
1747 : Alice Hodgson [21:6:1747] and Hannah Hodgson,[11:7:1747]
1748 : Elizabeth Raw [21:9:1748]
1750 : Margaret Akrigg [20:1:1750/1], Robert Akrigg [7:1:1750]
1755 : Mary Hodgson [13:11:1755]
1756 : Margaret Hodgson [21:2:1756], John Hodgson [9:9:1756]
       The record adds of him 'He was a worthy young man
       having a good gift of the ministry'.
       John Raw (of Garsdale) [21:3:1756].
1757 : Sarah Raw (wife of John) [23:4:1757], George Raw
       [13:5:1757]
1759 : (Agnes, daughter of James Winn; 16:3:1759). Her sister
       Tabitha was died 3 days later [19:3:1759]. Agnes
       was 'not in unity'. (Nor was Mary Buck (nee Dawson)
       17:4:1759).
1760 : Margaret Hodgson, [27:10:1760]
1766 : Michael Akrigg (of Round Ing) [4:7:1766], Elizabeth,
       his wife, [5:10:1766]
1767 : Mary Winn, daughter of James Winn [22:9:1767]
1768 : (Edward Raw (not in unity) 1:1:1768, and his wife,
       Elizabeth.)

1769 : Sarah Raw, second wife of John Raw, [23:2:1769]
       (Mary Winn, w of James Winn)
1771 : Thomas Raw, [31:12:1771/2]
1772 : Rebecca Davis, wife of Aaron Davis. [7:10:1772] and
       William Hodgson of Garsdale [16:7:1772) small pox.
1774 : (Elizabeth Akrigg (nee Alderson), Mabel Alderson
       [26:3:1774], Mary Clemmy [27:2:1774]
1777 : Thomas Winn of Reacha ('an ancient and valueable Publick
       friend'), perhaps 90 years old, [17:4:1777].
       John Raw [2:9:1777].(James Winn (son of Thomas)
       (1:5:1777) 'not in unity'.)
1778 : (Mabel Richardson (10:3:1778) 'not in unity')
1779 : Joshua Alderson [18:4:1779], Esther Winn [11:8:1779].
1780 : (Aaron Davies (of East Houses) (6:1:1780) not in unity)
1781 : (Elizabeth Akrigg, (w. of Robert of Aldershaw)
       (17:4:1781) 'not in unity'). See 1815 and 1843.
1783 : Thomas Lund, of Grisdale, was buried (20:4:1783) at
       Leayate, Dent.
1785 : Isabell Alderson, (wife of Joshua Alderson Snr (aged 87)
       [17:9:1785]
1786 : (John Raw (31:1:1789) Not in unity.)
1787 : (Emme Raw (6:3:1786) not in unity)
1788 : (Agnes Winn (31:8:1788) not in unity)
1792 : Edmund Winn of Fea Fow (61) [22:3:1792]. (Deborah
       his wife)'. (Samuel Lund, and his wife, Elizabeth
       were both buried at Leayate)
1800 : (Samuel and Elizabeth Davis), Mary Winn of Howshaw-
       Head [27:1:1800]. (Edward Raw (22:1:1800) 'not
       in unity').
1812 : Ann Akrigg [23:2:1812]
1815 : (Robert Achrigg (of Aldershaw, aged 83) (19:3:1815) not
       in unity. He built the present building).
1817 : John Raw [4:7:1817]
1821 : (Agnes Lund daughter of James Lund (24:5:1821),
       (Margaret Davis, widow of Aaron Davis 27:6:1821)
1822 : (Agnes Thompson, widow of John Thompson 15:2:1822),
       (Aron Davis, son of Samuel Davis 8:3:1822)
1823 : (Thomas Winn 19:10:1823)
1824 : (Edmund Winn was buried at Garsdale 'he was a minister
       some time'.)
1826 : (William Hodgson 1:8:1826)
1827 : (Mary Davis 6:12:1827)
1829 : (Thomas Aldershaw), and Elizabeth, [13:5:1829] (his wife
       aged 76 of Scale).
1843 : (Elizabeth Achrigg (spinster), Aldershaw, aged 71.
1860 : (Samuel Davies of Aldershaw, 81 years of age).
1861 : (Deborah Davies of High Ing, Spinster 83, born Scale.)
1863 : (Betty Davies, wife of Samuel, aged 75)

. . . . .

Source : Public Record Office, London. RG 6 / 1197.

June 4th 1677

In the name of god amen I Reynold Winn of Grisdale neab in body but in perfect mind and memory praised be god, doe make this my last will and testament in maner and forme as followes Imprimis I doe give to my wife Mabell Winn halfe of all my good exepting rushes bedstocks tables and bords they may remaine in the houses untill the death of my wife and then to goe with the houses and orchards to them it is ordered for. Item...

THE OPENING AND CLOSING PASSAGES OF THE WILL OF REYNOLD WINN, 1677.

Reynold Harrison.
Antony Mason
John Winn
James Burton

witnesses

Witnes my hand

Collato facta fideli concordat hac copia cu Originali Testo... in Manu Anthonij Mason et per me Examinal p mr

Anthony Mason

Rich: Trotter
Ns: Pub:

I John Close Junior in Grysdale, in ye Parish of Sedbergh & County of York being in health, & perfect in mind & memory, for wch I am thankfull to ye Lord, and being for a Journey, & not knowing when my Return may be, nor ye time of my departure out of ys Life, do make & ordaine this my last Will & testament, in manner & form following. First I Committ My Soule to God, my ffaithfull Creator, who gave itt, and my Body to ye Earth to be Desently Buried, at ye Charg of my Executer hereafter named, and my temporall Estate wherewith it hath pleased God to Bless me, I order & dispose of as followeth. Imprimis, Its my will & mind that all my just Debts, Legacyes & ffunerall Expences be payed & discharged by my Executrix out of ...

THE OPENING AND CLOSING PASSAGES OF THE WILL OF JOHN CLOSE, JUNIOR, 1715.

this my Will performed & for their care & pains theirin I give to Each of them Six shillings, Item I give to my maidservant Elisabeth Hugginson one pound & lastly I do Establish this to be my last Will & Testament in witness whereof I have hereunto put my hand & seale in ... in presence this 8th day of ye second month called April In ye Yeare 1715 in ye sight & presence of

michaell Dawson
William ... solemnly affirmed.

John   Close

QUAKERS AND METHODISTS

By the nineteenth century the Quakerism of the dale was in decline and Methodism took over. The enthusiasm had abated. John Wesley, the founder of Methodism, wrote of the Quakers he knew :

> 'Ye are weak and become like other men. The Lord is well nigh departed from you. Where is now the spirit, the life, the power?' (1)

He opposed many Quaker beliefs and practices as they infected his Methodist Societies but he admired many individual Quakers, and this admiration was mutual. Quaker doctors attended to him personally, and Methodism benefitted from Quaker generosity.

In the earliest days of Methodism the quietism of the Quakers had invaded the London societies and Wesley had moved to oppose it. As the century wore on, wherever he had the chance, he baptised Quakers and received them into Methodism. This movement, however, was not all in one direction. In 1775 Ralph Mather, a Methodist preacher, reported at Loughborough :

> 'near twenty have turned off Methodism to the Quakers. As this is the case, prejudice may shut up their hearts, except to those who can speak "thee" and "thou" and wear a broad brimmed hat, and who have learned their phrases'.
> (2)

For the rest of Wesley's life, till his death in 1791, it was a war of attrition and of pamphlets. Robert Barclay, the Quaker, wrote his 'Apology' and Wesley replied with his 'Further Appeal to men of reason and religion'.

In 1781 Wesley described the early Quaker societies as being 'composed mostly of persons that seemed disordered in their brains' (3) but added in a letter at the same time 'I love and esteem many of the present Quakers'. (4)

Some Quakers had been generous to the early Methodists and had been present in considerable numbers in Wesley's open air meetings. Often enough the Methodist preachers used a Quaker field for their meeting when the parish church was closed to them; and, when attacked by the mob, could anticipate Quaker support and rescue, for the Quakers were also a persecuted people.

In 1743, when Wesley had begun to build the Orphan House in Newcastle, and had only twenty-six shillings in his pocket, a wealthy Quaker wrote to him :

'Friend Wesley,

I have had a dream concerning thee. I thought I saw thee surrounded with a large flock of sheep, which thou didst not know what to do with. My first thought after I woke was, that it was thy flock in Newcastle, and that thou hadst no house of worship for them. I enclose a note for one hundred pounds, which may help thee to provide a house'. (5)

Wesley particularly admired Quaker simplicity and commended it to the Methodist people when, in 1760, he preached to them about dress :

'Two things I particularly remarked among them - plainness of speech, and plainness of dress. I willingly adopted both, with some restrictions, and particularly plainness of dress'. (6)

He was also very impressed with Quaker work among the poor, and with their schools, and it was a Quaker book on the slave trade which moved Wesley to become a powerful advocate of its abolition.

On the other hand Wesley challenged the Quakers as to whether their practice of 'theeing' and 'thouing' everyone, or refusing to uncover their heads and refusing to take oaths was not 'to make religion stink in the nostrils of infidel and heathen' (7) and he asked whether their plainness had degenerated into an outward form? They had become, he believed, narrow-minded 'mistaking the sample for the whole bale of cloth'. (8) He thought that beneath their simplicity there was something more reprehensible :

'What multitudes of you are very jealous as to the colour and form of your apparel (the least important of all the circumstances that relate to it), while in the most important, the expense, they are not concerned at all. They will not put on scarlet or crimson stuff, but the richest velvet, so it be black or grave. They will not touch a coloured riband, but will cover themselves with a stiff silk from head to foot. They cannot wear purple; but make no scruple at all of being clothed in fine linen; yea, to such a degree, that the linen of the Quakers is grown almost a proverb.

Surely you cannot be ignorant, that the sinfulness of fine apparel lies chiefly in the expensiveness; in that it is robbing God and the poor; it is defrauding the fatherless and the widow; it is wasting the food of the hungry, and witholding his raiment from the naked to consume it on our own lusts'. (9)

Wesley was to say later of his Methodists that their hard work and honesty would make them rich and he feared this more than their enemies. But, for the time being, in 1772, he wrote to Mary Stokes :

'Go not near the tents of those dead, formal, men called Quakers' (10)

It was not, however, great wealth which overcame the Quakerism of Grisdale. In that secluded area, at high altitude, with harsh winters and uncertain summers it took all their hard work and ingenuity to wring a modest living from the land. If they did well, as some did, it was to their credit.

As well as attacks from without, and the attraction some Quakers found in the enthusiasm of Methodism, the Quakers had a problem from within. This added to their undoing. The record of the Brigflatts monthly meeting gives us ample evidence of the way Quaker families were marrying into each other, and we have seen how intermingled the Grisdale families became. At one of the early meetings, held in the house of John Denison in 1679 it was declared :

'this day being the 29th of the 2nd month: did John Winn of Grisdale lay before friends againe his Intention of marriage with Margaret Regnoldson daughter to Arthur Regnoldson and ffriends finding nothing but clearness every way thereon and both fathers being there present haveing signified their satisfaction in their proceeding accordingly, ffriends did give their consent, being well satisfied therein, that they may go on to accomplish the same, as in the wisdome of God'. (11)

Obviously there was nothing in such a marriage to cause Friends any concern. Both parties were members of the society, as well as the fathers who were there to agree. However, for a society as closely packed, and closely knit, as the society of the dale there were other problems.

The quarterly meeting of all the local meetings held at Kendal in November 1680 had been asked for a judgement on consanguinity, and near kinship in marriage. The meeting declared that, though they felt free of outward restraints, God's law forbade marriage between close relatives. It went on to warn that, when a marriage was about to take place, the couple concerned should not live in the same house until it was consummated. Nor should single men and women co-habit, even innocently, 'that in all things we may honour the God of truth'.

In the Brigflatts minute book for two years later there is a full report of a Westmoreland quarterly meeting of Friends which gave a considered judgement of how a young male Friend might approach a girl in marriage. Four points were made : that he should first lay the matter before the Lord; second that he should next approach her parents; thirdly that he should find out if any other Friend had proposals of marriage towards her and withdraw if that was the case, and fourthly, if the woman did not agree she should say so in writing and so leave him free to go elsewhere. In all this she does not seem to have been consulted until towards the end of the proceedings, but no doubt young Friends in those days (as now) had ways of keeping each other informed. Later in the minute book the girl is given the right to be consulted earlier in the process.

The fact that the Quarterly District minute was recorded in the Sedbergh minute book was because it was considered formative for every meeting in the neighbourhood, and the record was to be kept :

> 'with other papers formally given forth touching marriage and other necessary directions given forth by our Ancient Brethren touching affairs of the Church of Christ; and that all may be carefull in observing the same to the praise of Truth and Honour of God, who is worthy for ever.' (12)

The strict discipline applied by the Ancient Brethren was, in some ways, the strength of the Quakers, but it was also a weakness. Cupid found it difficult to fit into the pattern and young friends chafed against the bonds. Reading the Sedbergh minute book we see just such a case of discontent. It is the same problem of marriage outside the society which we found in the Grisdale Preparative meeting minutes. The Sedbergh book reads on April 27th 1703 :

> 'Joseph Baines (Snr) and John Sayrey were desired once more to speak to Isabell Ward about her disorderly (conduct) concerning herselfe in relation to marriage with a man of another society on account of religion (;) which they have accordingly done yet all takeing no place noe of late hath it any prevalancy with her, but she hath gone on to accomplishmt thereof (.) it is the sense and agreement of this meeting that she be publickly denied. It is the sense of this meeting that such as goe out from us for wife or husband or fall into other things scandalous & go (, are) worth(y) of open condemnation and there upon are denied; that Friends confirm what they have done, by their carriage and behaviour towards them that they may see their friends stande at a distance from them (,) allsoe aftersuch deniale if they shall confidently come to our meetings as if they had not done a mischief they shall be discretely advised'. (13)

So the discipline was applied, and continued so to be. Three months later the meeting asked :

'As touching women wearing bonnets, its desired that a question be moved at the quly meeting whether any should be worn or nay, withall it being the sense of this meeting rather not to wear any'. (14)

These passages are within fifty years of the beginning of the Quaker movement, and there is a long way to go before Methodism took over in Grisdale, but the seeds of discontent were there. The Quakers did not disapprove of marriage altogether, as did the Shaker people of the USA (who eventually died out because of this prohibition), but they restricted it so closely within the Quaker family that there were bound to be failures. It is said that nationally the Quakers declined to less that 20,000 members because of this, until the regulations were changed in 1859. No wonder the Quaker, Dr John Rutty, could write in his diary :

'The Methodists outstrip the quite, and consequently must advance beyond thee. I will catch a little of their fire, so help, Lord'. (15)

It is refreshing to find, in contrast to all this and in the same minute book in 1705, a regulation forbidding Quakers to kill 'Fish, viz salmon and trout in the breeding time' or 'follow or hunt the hair (hare) with a pack of hounds'. Good scriptural and ecological reasons were given for these prohibitions as well as pointing to the offence that such 'lightness of mind' would give to the enemies of the professors of truth.

It is also pleasant to think of salmon breeding in the upper reaches of the Clough river in 1705, and even, perhaps, in Grisdale Beck.

· · · · ·

1: Wesley's 'Works' VIII 189.
2: Letter to Henry Brook. See Walton's 'Notes..for..a biography of William Law' pp 596-6.
3: Wesley 'Concise Ecclesiastical History'.
4: Wesley 'Letters' VIII 252.
5: Moore's 'Wesley' I p550.
6: Wesley's 'Works' 3rd ed (ed Jackson) Vol XI 466-8.
7: Wesley 'Further Appeal'.
8: Wesley's 'Works' VIII 185.
9: Wesley 'Works' 3rd ed.(ed T. Jackson) Vol VIII 186.
10: Wesley : Letters : V 198-9.
11: Minutes of Brigflatts Monthly Meeting : WDFC F.
12: As 12.
13: As 12.
14: As 12.
15: Wesley Hist. Soc. Proceedings : VII 54.

Quarterly Meeting Resolution.

"At the Quarterly Meeting of the Sedbergh Circuit, held at Sedbergh on Thursday, December 27th 1889 (the Rev. W. Beales in the chair) consent was given to erect a Wesleyan Methodist Chapel at Grisedale. Steps to be taken at once towards securing a proper site."

IV - Mr. John Dent was unanimously appointed to the office of chapel Steward and Treasurer.

V - The Meeting decided to leave all arrangements for the Opening to the Committee.

William Beales

Stone-Laying.— The memorial Stone of Grisedale Wesleyan Chapel was laid on Thursday, May 30th 1889, by Mr. Joshua Dugdale on behalf of Mrs. Atkinson who was unable to attend. Address by Rev. Jabez Chambers of Middleham. A meeting was held in the evening in the Friends Meeting House — a most dilapidated building which had been occupied by the Wesleyans for many years. Addresses given by the Rev. F. Law, of Kirkby Stephen, & Rev. W. Beales; also by Mr. Joshua Dugdale & his fellows. Chairman—Mr. J. H. Wilson. It was a very wet & stormy day. Service, considering the day, well attended.

Opening.— The above Chapel was opened on Thursday, August 15th 1889, by the Rev. Geo Abbott, Chairman of the District, who preached in the afternoon on "The Day of Visitation"— Luke XIX. 41, 42. Evening Meeting addressed by Revs. W. J. Chant, of Lancaster, J. Dugdale, of Brindle, & W. Beales; also by Mr. Joshua Dugdale who gave the financial statement. Mr. J. H. Wilson Chairman. This also was a very wet & uncomfortable day. Chapel well filled.

William Beales

From the
GRISDALE
WESLEYAN
CHAPEL
TRUSTEES
MINUTE
BOOK
1889.

102

THE METHODISTS, The Great Inundation, and the Settle to Carlisle Railway

Methodism's entry into the area was, at first, laboured. George Whitefield had preached at Kendal in 1745, as the Young Pretender retreated northwards, but, despite several visits by John Wesley between 1753 and his death in 1791, no Methodist society was established in Kendal until 1795 under the ministry of a layman, Stephen Brunskill. From Kendal the Methodist witness spread out slowly in several directions into what was called the 'Dales Circuit'. It went to Ambleside, then Kirby Stephen and then up the valleys to Ravenstonedale and Garsdale Head. All this was under the care of only one or two ministers who had to ride the 'circuit' (that is the area in which their preaching places were), or walk it, as best they could.

It has always been part of Methodism's genius that it has used the gifts of lay people. Ministers were 'travelling' preachers in that they travelled from circuit to circuit; but lay preachers were 'local' preachers in that they served the circuit in which they lived. The preaching plan of 'The Wesleyan-Methodist Preachers in the Kendal Circuit' for the months of November 1847 to May 1848 lists Grisdale as one of the 28 preaching places. A service was held there every Sunday morning at 10am. In Garsdale there were three chapels, but there was none in Grisdale until 1889. In all probability the people met in the Quaker meeting house. Garsdale had three local preachers : Harper, Allen T. and Chapman. Grisdale had but one by the name of Tennant. The 1841 census returns list two Tennants in the dale and as it is likely at that time that the preacher would be the man of the house, we must choose between Christopher Tennant of East House (57 years of age in 1847) and Harry Tennant of Fea Fow (who was 37 in 1847). Both were farmers. By 1851 Christopher Tennant was at Reacher; while Harry Tennant was at Mousesyke. Both appear in the 1861 census. By 1871 Ann, the wife of Christopher, is described as an 'annuitant' and a border, aged 76, with the Couper family at Aldershaw. Nothing tells us which was the preacher.

As time went on Grisdale was linked with Sedbergh where a chapel had been built in 1805; and by the late 1850's Sedbergh and Hawes were linked together as one circuit, a link which was severed in 1871. An octagonal chapel was built at Sedbergh in 1865 and saw the remarkable work of the Rev. William Moister who had returned from overseas and built up the churches, and provided a house, at his own expense, for the minister. (1)

When the turnpike was built along the fell sides in 1761 it ran from Sedbergh to Hawes past the turning into Grisdale. Part of it survives as 'Grisdale old road' to this day, and on that road is Grouse Hall where Richard Atkinson lived. Here is an extract from THE CRAVEN HERALD for February 11th 1971 :

'Richard Atkinson was a gamekeeper. He was a marvellous man, possessed of an iron will, and an even stronger faith, who died only 40 years of age, on the last day of May 1884.

During his all too short lifetime he conducted many missions throughout the district and was instrumental in furthering the cause of Methodism. One of these missions, held in the public hall, Sedbergh, went on for sixteen weeks and there were many converts.

Richard was also possessed of strong psychic qualities and could forecast with amazing accuracy how many converts there would be each night at his mission meetings. Often he would remain at home, engrossed in prayer, and his wife would attend the meeting. Upon her return he would tell her how many converts there had been, and he was invariably right. On one occasion at Hawes, when asked to forecast how many converts there would be at an evening meeting, he replied very cautiously 'one young lady'. Asked to describe her attire he did so in detail. A young lady did attend the meeting and was converted. She was dressed exactly as he had described her. Yet she had neither seen nor heard of him before and had arrived in the small country town only that very morning from London.

On another occasion, when preaching at the old Quaker chapel in Grisdale, he suddenly had a vision of a coffin being borne into the building with a certain name on the plate. Shortly after a lady of that name died and the funeral was held at the chapel.

Preaching every night of the week in Dent Head Chapel he would set out each evening on foot to walk over the formidable Rysell Fell which, exhilarating and delightful in sunshine, assumes a grim and sinister mantle at nightfall, with its treacherous black peat bogs which have claimed the life of more than one unwary traveller. Separating Garsdale from Cowgill and Dent the fell is a short route between dales and, after each meeting, he would retrace his steps in the dark with unerring accuracy and confidence born of experience. One night, as he was walking over the desolate and swampy Black Moss, he saw a vision of his mother envelopped in flames. We realise it could have been bog gas flaring up, but he clearly saw his mother in flames. The very next evening, as he set out to preach again, he instructed his daughters not to leave his mother's side. An invitation from up the dale proved to be too great an attaction for them and they ignored his plea. During his absence, his mother, alone in the house, fell on the fire and was burned to death.

A great friend of Mr Atkinson was the late Mr Joseph Henry Wilson. One day he set off to Hawes to do some shopping taking Richard with him. Arriving in the town he said to the tailor 'I want you to measure this fellow for a pair of breeches. He's worn t'knees out wi praying to keep ye fellas out of hell'. It was true enough for he had a habit of praying each morning at daybreak under a certain thorn tree, and, in the passage of time his knees had worn indentations in the ground'. (2)

The article went on to suggest that the local people built the Richard Atkinson Memorial Chapel, Grisdale, from the stones of the Quaker meeting house, doing the work themselves. For reasons given below I believe this story to be only partly true. What is more likely is that the stones of the meeting house were used to repair the river bank after flood damage.

The Grisdale Methodist Chapel minute book begins with a list of 65 subscribers to the building fund. Prominent are the names of Winn, Lund, Allen, Harper, Mason and Pratt some of which names we have met before. The same names are to be found in the area to this day. The total raised was £252:4:10 and this was laid out on various builders and the necessary materials. The value of voluntary labour was assessed at £47:7:0. The trustees promised to keep all things in order and signed their names :

William Handley	William Redmayne	Miles Atkinson
William Mason	James Allen Lund	Samuel Lund
George Mason	John Dent	Thomas Harper
John Lund	Richard Shaw	James Cowper
		Thomas Oldfield

The regular minutes, recording the building work, as it went on, tell us that walling cost 2/- a yard, slating was 7 pence a yard and the joinery, plumbing, glazing, plastering and painting cost £102. Preparations were made for the opening at which Richard Atkinson's youngest daughter was to be invited to lay a memorial stone. The necessary tea would cost 6 pence a person, and seat rents would be 6 pence a year. In a special minute the stone-laying and opening ceremonies were recorded :

'STONE-LAYING : the memorial Stone of Grisedale Wesleyan Chapel was laid on Thursday, May 30th 1889 by Mr Joshua Dugdale on behalf of Mrs Atkinson who was unable to attend. Address by Rev. Jabes Chambers of Middleham. A meeting was held in the evening at the Friends Meeting House - a most dilapidated building which had been used by the Wesleyans for many years - address given by the Rev F. Law of Kirby Stephen, and Rev W. Beales: also by Mr Joshua Dugdale and his father. Chairman - Mr J. H. Wilson. It was a very wet and stormy day. Services, considering the day, well attended.

OPENING : The above Chapel was opened on Thursday, August 15th 1889 by the Rev Geo. Abbott, Chairman of the District, who preached in the afternoon on 'The Day of

Visitation' - Luke XIX 41, 42. Evening meeting addressed
by Rev W.I. Chant of Lancaster, J. Dugdale of Oundle, and
W. Beales; also by Mr Joshua Dugdale who gave the
financial statement. Mr J.H. Wilson Chairman. This also
was a very wet and uncomfortable day. Chapel well filled.

William Beales'   (3)

The memorial stone was at the apex of the gable, just under
the point of the roof so the chapel was nearly completed when
it was laid. It is now in Garsdale 'Street Chapel' graveyard.
The fact that a meeting could be held the same night at the
Quaker meeting house suggests that the building must still have
ben intact, however dilapidated.

It is not surprising that the Chairman of the Methodist
District spoke of the 'Day of Visitation'. It was a timely
message, but the weather which blighted the stone-laying and
opening was not reserved for the Methodists alone. Only a week
before, at midday on Wednesday the 8th of August, a torrent of
water had carried away bridges, walls, trees and fences in
Garsdale. It was a wonder that those who spoke at the opening
could reach the dale at all. Garsdale itself on the 8th of
August was all unsuspecting, for no rain had fallen on it. In
Grisdale it was calculated that 4½ inches of rain fell in three
hours, and equivalent of 250 tons an acre. This water poured
down the river bed destroying the road, uprooting trees,
flooding houses, depositing sand and mud on the fields and
spoiling hay in the fields.

Mr John Lund, of Roger Pot, told me that his father, William
Lund, as a boy of 13, witnessed the bursting of the ground high
up in Grisdale which started the flood. This is how he
described it to Chris Pratt :

'it was just on noon and I was sheltering under some rocks
away the other side of Round Ing. On my own I was and I
have never seen such rain. It was thundering too. Anyway,
I just happened to look out further west, to see if there
was a break to it anywhere, when I saw the ground
beginning to rise up about two or three hundred yards
away. Like a great blister it was. Well I didn't know what
to think. More and more the ground rose until nearly three
acres had come up to four or five feet in height. And then
it burst with a terrible noise, and a big wave came. A
real torrent it was, carrying away sods and rocks into the
valley'.

A letter was written to the Yorkshire Post and widely copied
asking for help, especially from land owners. There was little
response and the Vicar of Garsdale, the Rev. Allton, added a
final comment in the appeal committee minute book : (4)

'not one of them either gave one penny, or assisted in
raising one penny to help their poorer brethren, except
Mrs Batty who has always shown her sympathy with the poor
of the dale.'

Before the water reached Garsdale it had carried away bridges
at Scale, Fea Fow and Blakemire. It is still possible to see in
certain places on the river bank the abutments of bridges which
have disappeared for, some of them, especially if they were
made of wood, were never replaced. A sum of £75 was paid out in
total to farmers in Grisdale. These were William Throupe of
Round Ing, John Dent of Scale, Mr Lund of Fea Fow, Rowland
Harper of Reacher, Miles Atkinson of Moorrigg, T. Harper of
Mousesyke, Mr Cowper of Roan Tree and James Allen of Blakemire.
Very much larger sums were paid out in Garsdale.

It seems that the bad weather of 1889 was typical of the last
years of the nineteenth century. In July 1899 there was another
inundation which missed Grisdale, but wrecked Hardraw village
and damaged the waterfall. Such wetness made it hard for small
farms to survive, where late haymaking was a necessity, and
smaller farms were amalgamated. High Lathe, High Flust, High
Ing were absorbed, West Scale joined East Scale and Rowantree,
Reacher and Hawshawhead were under threat.

Recently the census forms for 1841 to 1881 have been
available, and they prove what has always been understood :
that farms were small, families large and most farmers did
something else as well as farm. The 1841 census is sparse in it
information, and gives no occupation other than 'farmer'. I
give the farm names as in the documents :   (5)

At BLAKEMIRE lived William and Ann AKRIGG with 4 children.
At ROANTREE lived Joshua and Nancy DAVIS with 5 children and a
          manservant.
At ALDERSHAW was Samuel DAVIS, 2 daughters and Betty AKRIGG.
At HIGH ING were Deborah DAVIS and Deborah THOMPSON.
At EAST HOUSE were John and Mary THOMPSON nand 5 children. Also
          Christopher and Ann TENNANT and Thomas ALLISON a shoe
          maker's apprentice.
At HOWSHAW HEAD lived Mary THOMPSON and 3 grown children.
At FEAFALL lived Harry and Isabell TENNANT and 3 children.
At FLUST lived William HODGSON and 3 children.
At ROUND ING lived Robert and Ann AKRIGG, 4 children and 2
          other adults.
At FARSCALE lived James and Betty BURTON, 3 children and an
          agricultural labourer.
At NEARSCALE lived Ralph and Betty BLADES and 2 older people.
At REACHER lived Betty TENNANT with 2 teenagers.
At MOOR RIDGE lived John GREENBANK with his mother and 6
          children.
At MOUSE SIKE lived John and Betty LUND and 5 others.

This was a total of 79 people in the dale, of whom 49 were aged 20 years or under. In the 1851 census there is not much extra information, but :

At BLAKEMIRE lived the AKRIGGS
At RANTREE lived the DAVIS family on 90 acres.
At ALDERSHAW lived DAVIS, BIRTLES and HARPER on 9 acres.
At MOORIGS lived the GREENBANKS on 74 acres.
At HIGHING the THOMPSON's and DAVIS's on 25 acres.
At EAST HOUSES the THOMPSON's. Master shoemakers.
At HOWSHAWHEAD the THROUPES on 40 acres.
At FEAFALL the LUNDS on 60 acres.
At LOWFLUST the THOMPSONS, farm labourers.
At HIGHFLUST the AKRIGGS, farm labourers.
At SCALE the BURTONS and BLADES.
At REACHEA Christopher TENNANT with 20 acres.
At MOSSIKE Henry TENNANT with 90 acres.

Two houses were empty. There were several knitters, an errand girl and a coal miner. Of 87 people in the dale 42 were 20 years of age and under. In 1861 we find :

BLAKEMIRE (Richard Blades) had 18 acres.
REANTREE was occupied by James Burton, labourer.
ALDERSHAW (Nancy Davis) had 97 acres.
HIGHING (Deborah Davis) had 14 acres.
EAST HOUSE (Rowland Harper) had 30 acres.
HOUSAHEAD (Joshua Thompson) had 40 acres.
FEAFAW (Samuel Lund) had 66 acres.
FLUST was empty.
ROUNDING (William Throupe) had 100 acres.
One of the SCALE houses was empty.
REACHER (Christopher Tennant) had 80 acres.
MOOR RIGG (Richard Burton) had 100 acres.
MOUSE SIKE (Henry Tennant) had 107 acres.
SCALE (Thomas Metcalf). No acreage given.

There were 68 people in the dale, of whom 38 were 20 years of age or under. The Friends Meeting House is noted. There was a carter and a shepherd, as well as 'farmers'.

In 1871 there were 71 people in the dale and the building of the Settle to Carlisle railway had not gone un-noticed. 1871 was only the beginning of the building programme which drove a fast, all-weather, route up the spine of England. By 1881, our next census available, the work was over. The 72 mile route was driven through tunnels, and over viaducts, at the cost of immense labour and much suffering. It is said that dozens of infant bodies lie buried under the wall of the Frostrow Chapel graveyard, the result, no doubt, of the hard and meagre conditions, and the consequent illness, in the shanty towns built to accommodate the 'navvies' and their families. At the height of 'railway mania' 2000 people lived in these 'towns', and at Chapel le Dale more than 200 of them were buried in the graveyard, victims of small pox, alcohol or the violent wind which in winter blew them off the half-finished viaducts on which they were working.

There were some tough and rough characters who took part in the drunken fights on Black Moss at the head of Garsdale, but the local Christian Churches did their best to 'improve the time'. Services were held in huts and chapels and even in railway waiting rooms when they had been built. Special evangelists were appointed to minister to the shanty families and, in the Garsdale section of the census, more that one person indicated his Christian status, as, for example, 'Primitive Methodist Local Preacher'. Richard Atkinson, then in his 20's, would have been hard at work among them. No preacher appears as a lodger in the Grisdale section of the census. 1871 was too early in the story, and the walk from Grisdale would be too long for those sections of the line under construction in that year. However :

Robert CAPSTICK, a road labourer, lived at WHIT HEAD with his wife, Elizabeth, a dress maker.

Alexander MACKINTOSH and John MACGILLIRAY (railway masons) and Doncan FRANCIS (a railway labourer) lived with the GEAR family.

ALDERSHAW was occupied by John ATKINSON. His son was a stone mason.

Otherwise : the THROUPs were at BLACK MIRE, the HAYGARTHs at EAST HOUSE, the THOMPSOPNs at HAWSHA HEAD, Samuel LUND at FAFAW, William TROUP at ROUND ING, Richard WILKINSON at SCALE, John METCALF at the other SCALE house, the HARPERS at REACHSHAW Richard BURTON at MORERIG, John RAW at RANTREE, William DENT at MOUSESYKE where also was James LUND and family. There were 74 people in the dale of whom 35 were 20 years of age and under.

In 1881 everyone was farming. Here is the record :

MOUS-SIKE : Thomas and Isabella RIDDING, 6 children.
RONETREE : Richard and Ann WILKINSON, 5 children.
MOOR-RIGG : James and Elizabeth BURTON, 3 children.
REACHA : Rowland and Betty HARPER, 7 children.
SCALE : William and Mary HOLME, 2 children, a servant.
The other Scale house was unoccupied.
ROUND ING : William and Ann THROUP, 3 children.
FLUST : Michael and Mary THOMPSON, one child.
FEA-FAW : James and Isabella LUND, 5 children, a servant.
          Also Samuel and Agnes LUND.
HOUSHA HEAD : Elizabeth THOMPSON, with 4 in family.
ALDERSHAW : Rowland and Mary COWPER., 4 children.
BLAKEMIRE : James and Maru ALLEN, 6 children. Also William
            and Ann BANKS with one child.

There were 80 people in the dale of whom 50 were aged 20 and under. Obviously the dale throbbed with life. It was a poor, but vital, place to live in.

The more recent occupancies of the houses are as follows:

ROUND ING	: B. Pratt to 1935	Nr SCALE	: J. Dent c 1905
	: J. Pratt 35-45		: W. Lund 1906-23
	: Baines 43-6		: T. Harper 23-45
	: R. Harper 46-7		: R. Thwaite 45-53

EAST HO	: J. Allen c 1910	FEA FOW	: W. Harper after 1920
	: D. Allen c 1915		: G. Thornbro 33-42
	: J.W. Allen 1940's		: J. Thornbro 1942
	: N. Thompson 1950's		: G. Wallace 1940's
	: The Garnetts 1980's		

MOORRIGG	: W. Thwaite 1916	ALDERSHAW	: Atkinson c 1916
	: J. Thwaite 25-7		: R. Harper 1930's
	: J. Lund 27-33		: J. Harper
	: Thornbro till 1940's		: J. Mason 36-7
			: restored 1986

MOUSESYKE : T. Harper 1916, J. Thwaite 1940 onwards, 1960' the Gibsons.

The meagre chapel records show that, as well as a place of worship, it was a communal centre for the dale. Almost everyone belonged to the chapel and joined in the tea parties and outings. Lamp oil, varnish, cement and coal were bought, and paint was put on the windows.

The Primitive Methodist Church, which began in 1807, also had preaching in Grisdale dating from 1850. It was in the Middleham circuit and there was a fortnightly service. A plan of 1872 has G.Yare and A.Yare, of High Ing, as preachers, and R. Wilkinson (of Far Scale) and J. Raw were prayer leaders. Perhaps the services were held at High Ing and Far Scale.

On September 22nd 1915 the Wesleyan Chapel trust was renewed. Miles Atkinson, William Mason, Michael Thompson, Joshua Dugdale, George Mason, Joseph Henry Wilson, John Lund, William Redmayne, James Allen Lund and Richard Shaw had died out of the original trustees. The continuing trustees were :

Thomas Harper   William Lund   Richard Allen
William Thwaite   John Lund   Bell Pratt, and they were all described as 'Farmer, Grisdale'. (6)

I remember Chris Pratt telling a party, who were visiting Grisdale, of his conversion many years before in the chapel, and of his devotion, and the devotion of the dale's people, to the chapels of the dales. It would be impossible, and un-necessary, to try to reproduce the material he supplied which is to be found in THE DALE THAT DIED, published in 1975 by J.M. Dent, and written by Barry Cockcroft. It is no longer in print, but may be found in libraries.

Instead, I have sought to speak to those who knew the dale in their youth, and are still alive as I write. The last Methodist farmer in the dale was Mr Jack Thwaite, who farmed Mouse Syke. He recalled filling Beck House with hay, working with a hay sledge. His sister, Mrs Allen, and her daughter were the last remaining members of the chapel in 1972 when it closed for worship. It was to Jack Thwaite that the people of the nearby dales turned when a pig was to be killed. He charged five shillings for doing the job. He liked the fat, and 'Duke' Harper of Mousesyke often had the pig's feet.

The Rev. James Alderson was a joiner before he left the dales to enter the Methodist ministry. In his retirement he has made scale models of all the implements formerly used by farmers in the dales. These may be seen in the Upper Dales Museum at Hawes, and give a vivid picture, to those who have eyes to see, of dales life a hundred years ago.

Mr G. Spencer, who became a local preacher in 1922 told me he belonged to the Wesleyan circuit. Before Methodist Union in 1932 the Primitive Methodist places of worship were : Street Chapel Garsdale, Cotterdale, Milthrop, Deepdale and there was also a PM chapel in Dent.

As well as worship in chapels, services were also held in houses. He remembered preaching in Middleton Hall which had mullioned windows, original panelling and a large fireplace. The thought came to him during the service that perhaps the last time worship had been conducted there was in the sixteenth century when a Catholic priest surreptitiously celebrated mass.

When he began to preach only one circuit member had a car. He was Richard Harper, the grand-father of the present Richard Harper. Everyone else walked or cycled. The minister had a motor-bike. 'Today' he said, the preacher turns up in his car, and after the service has a chat at the gate and drives away. In those days you were planned for a double, afternoon and evening, and you spent the time between services having a sumptuous tea at Mrs Harper's at Mousesyke. The dales people were poor but generous'. There would be 25 to 30 children in the congregation, for all but one family in the dale came to the chapel.

It was the custom to hold a prayer meeting after the evening service. 'If you were devout' said Mr Spencer 'you knelt; the Catholics wer'nt in it in those days'. Some would pray quietly but 'With the menfolk it was one big shout from beginning to end'. He added 'there would be a fair amount of responding - hear, hear, aye, aye, and groans'. One minister's wife went to a service at Grisdale for the first time with her husband, and, when the congregation knelt down they disappeared from her view behind the pews. After the service she asked her husband 'Frank what were all those animals making a noise outside the chapel for?' He must have laughed all the way home.

Mr Spencer added 'They were brought up in the good Methodist tradition, they had no fear of death. They had a sound social conscience, their elderly relatives and maiden aunts finished their time with the young folk looking after them. They put their religion into practice alright'.

Mr Jack Dawson, of Sedbergh, wrote an account for me of 'A double in Grisdale'. Here are some extracts from it :

'Looking eastward from Sedbergh town, beyond the enormous land-mass of Baugh Fell, there is a valley whose quietness is broken only by the plaintive cry of the curlew or the bleat of a sheep. This is Grisdale, the cul-de-sac valley which at one time afforded a living to sixteen families. Today it is very different, the actors have departed, the props have been dismantled and the play is over. Even the box-office, the Chapel, has suffered 'change of use'.

My grand-father, William Dawson, was a Methodist Local Preacher before the turn of the century, and frequently preached at Grisdale. He normally walked from Sedbergh, but I am aware that he owned a 'penny-farthing' bicycle. My father, John Michael Dawson, became a Local Preacher in 1909 and was active for 60 years. In the late 1920's our home in Sedbergh would be gladdened by my mother's announcement, as she examined each new preaching plan : 'Dad has a double in Grisdale'. This meant that either my brother or myself would accompany Dad on the cross-bar of his bike. Why were we so delighted? Because the Grisdale people were always glad to see us and they made us so welcome. To share the fellowship of their homes between the afternoon and evening service was an experience I do not wish to forget. Even today, after a passage of 60 years, these vivid memories come flooding back. I used to think that Grisdale was like heaven - a place of bliss and happiness - not easily reached, for it was a long hard journey, up hill nearly all the way from Sedbergh town. It was a 'hard slog', but the welcome and rapture at the end of the journey was ample compensation.

My predominant memories of Grisdale are of spring and summer days. I well remember the wealth and variety of bird life during the nesting season, the myriads of summer flowers carpeting the valley bottom meadows, and the river flowing by. Perhaps the most thought-provoking memory I have of the valley was of an occasion when I went, as a boy, at the back end of the year, when the days were shortening and it was dark when the evening service started. Lights could be seen moving slowly from the distant farmsteads, down the hillsides, over the footpaths, through the fields, across the valley from all directions; slowly the lights were moving, all converging on the Chapel, for the Chapel was the very centre of valley life. Here they could sing together, worship together, pray together and here they could laugh and talk together for they were happy people. Sunday was a very special day in Grisdale, it was Chapel day. I thank God for a double in Grisdale'.

Mr John Lund was born at East Scale but left the dale at the age of two years. He would be invited back by his relatives to the Christmas parties which were held nightly in the different houses for a couple of weeks in the new year. 'It was a nightly round of visits, good food and games : the tables groaned with food, and there was great hilarity'. One year he arrived late at High Ing and found the company sitting round the room. They told him they had adopted a foreign custom of not shaking the hand 'but the foot'. As instructed he began to do this but, imagine his dismay when his hostess's 'leg' came away in his hand. He was not allowed to forget it for some time. The chapel, he said, was the centre of the life of the dale. Everybody went to everything. Camp meetings were held in the open air in the summer, and there was a 'May do' for the chapel anniversary. At harvest festival time there would a Saturday supper, two services on Sunday, a sale of goods and a feast. The people from Fell End would walk over from Uldale and stay to tea and supper before walking back.

So, the great 'chapel days' are still not forgotten. Not far away, in the gentler reaches of the lower dales, people still live who had a Grisdale childhood and, every year, some of them ride into the dale to have a look at the old place once again.

. . . . .

1: Bryer : A History of Methodism in Kendal, Kirby Lonsdale, and Sedbergh. Kendal 1987.
2: The Craven Herald and Pioneer : Skipton. February 1975.
3: The Minute Books of the Grisdale Methodist Church : which are deposited at the Cumbria Record Office.
4: Garsdale Inundation Fund : collection of documents in the Cumbria Record Office, Kendal : WPR/60.
5: Copies of the Census Records in the hands of the Sedbergh and District Historical Society.
6: Grisdale Methodist Church Minute Books, as above.

TODAY

From time to time a journalist visits Grisdale (usually for a day) and writes a sad little piece about the ruined houses and the beautiful, but empty, dale. He is inspired, no doubt, by the title of the book 'The Dale that Died'.

While it is true that the crowded homes of the last century are now empty it is far from true that the dale has 'died'. The flocks of children who once filled the dale may never return (except for a day) but several of the houses have been repaired, people 'come back' for summer visits, the land is thoroughly farmed, sheep are abundant and, above all, nature in all her forms is as rampant as ever she was. Because of the absence of pesticides, which have mutilated the flora and fauna of many parts of lowland Britain, we have seen things in Grisdale which are becoming scarce elsewhere.

For some time now we have kept a nature diary. Here are some excerpts from it :

* It is just after Christmas and the frost is hard upon the ground. It is colder here than it is in the city because we stand at 1200 feet' above sea level. The moon last night was full and bright and cast our shadow on the ground. With the total absence of street lamps, or even a glow from a distant town, we can see the stars as our ancestors must have seen them.

* We have had the tail of the hurricane which swept the rest of Britain. Torrential rain and thunder. The wind has badly damaged our summer house and the rising water table has lifted the floor at Beck House to that it will have to be relaid. Most dramatically the whole valley bottom was flooded as the river overflowed. Bow Bridge was an island in a flowing sea more than a foot deep. Fortunately those who first built the Chapel had seen this sort of thing before and chose their ground well. For some time the mole catcher has fought a losing battle against 'old mouldy warp', setting his traps and hanging more that 200 of their bodies on the barbed wire. Now the flood seems to have settled the matter, drowning out their underground citidels.

* It is late March and my wife went up to Grisdale on Friday night for the weekend leaving Manchester in the rain. As she reached Garsdale Head the rain turned to snow and she had to abandon the car on Grisdale old road. She walked the last mile with Mr Garnett who was going to East House. Neither of them noticed Two Hole Bridge, it was so covered over with snow. At Chapelhouse she swept a foot of it from the door before she could get in. Unfortunately, she realised at that point that she had left most of her food in the car. She phoned me to say

'don't come' and turned up the central heating. On Saturday it was still snowing and she made her way to Mousesyke to ask for some survival rations. It was still snowing when she went to bed. She woke on Sunday morning to hear the welcome drip of a thaw and walked out of the valley to find the road men with a JCB digging out the car. They helped her to start it and she came home. Make a note : buy a freezer.

* It is a Sunday morning in March. We are leaving at 7.00am to return to the city and it is barely light. As I stand at the door listening to the silence it is punctuated by the cry of a curlew returning from the sea-shore of south Wales or southern Ireland. He is flying high up the valley to establish his nesting site in the meadows and attract a mate. Spring is on its way.

* This May, as usual, the marsh marigolds cover the ground as with a cloth of gold. It used to be the custom for farmers to hang bunches of the flowers over their cattle byres to ward off witches and fairies. Perhaps these are what Shakespeare meant when he wrote of 'winking Mary buds'. The lambs are being born and the shepherd numbers them with paint as they come : 42, 43, 44, and constantly walks the meadow to ensure that they do not drown in the river. As they grow stronger they play together, leaping high in the air, and chasing each other across the fields.

* The meadowsweet is growing against the wall. The lady of the house used to cut this and strew it on the stone flagged floors because its sweet smell overcame any less desirable odours. There are also patches of nettle which we only partly discourage for they feed the caterpillers of small tortoise-shell and other butterflies which then feed on the buddleia. Earlier this year we found strong clumps of primroses and drifts of snowdrops on the banks of the road leading to the dale. The elder tree by Beck House is in flower. It is said that preachers used to tether their horses to that tree during a service at the chapel, and we once found a horseshoe in the ground nearby. I wonder if they allowed elderberry wine?

* When autumn comes a field mouse usually tries to move in with us. This we discourage, but the coming of spring brings out into the open, to the watchful eye, a number of small creatures. A weasel, like a bright-eyed brown pencil, makes his sinewy way in and out of the stones of a dry stone wall. A hare goes March mad in the open field. One early morning a rabbit and a heron stood within yards of each other on the open road before the heron went upstream to catch trout. One spring day, as we were repairing the roof, a buzzard dropped suddenly out of the sky into a field nearby and carried off a rat hidden in the grass to all but him. There are chickens in a nearby barn and where there is chicken food there can be rats. Those the buzzard does not get must be dealt with by the rat catcher.

THE SILENT STREAM

* One memorable dull May Monday we found an avocet in the
dale, probably blown off course and kept down by the lowering
clouds. We reported it to the local naturalists. They asked us
'are you sure it wasn't an oyster catcher?' We were sure, for
each year a pair of oyster catchers nest on the shingle bed
within our view on the bend of the river. Their eggs, if you
can find them, look like the stones among which they lie. If
you approach, the two adult birds walk ostentatiously away in
opposite directions, and then take to the wing in jagged and
noisy flight across the sky. When we finally persuaded the
naturalists to take us seriously they came ... on Saturday
morning. The sky had lifted on Friday night, and the avocet had
left.

* Last evening in the dusk I saw a barn owl quartering the
fields in front of the house in search of prey. There are
several old buildings in the neighbourhood which could provide
a nesting site such are denied to barn owls in other parts of
the country. Let us hope he finds a mate.

* Every spring for the last few years a sandpiper has nested
in our garden sitting tight upon her eggs so long as we did not
venture too near her. When she goes in search of food her
return approach is always the same. She lands on the wall at
the lower end of the garden and waits a while 'bob, bob,
bobbing' all the time. Then she walks along the wall until she
is opposite the nest, and flies in. The nest has four eggs each
with its narrower end pointing inwards. One year we were lucky
enough in the early morning to see the young hatch out. It
seemed only moments before they were up and running among the
flowers. Then they disappeared into the long grass not to be
seen again. It is incredible to think that in a matter of four
weeks they are quite independent and are able to follow their
parents back to South Africa.

* We have tried to record the names of the birds we have seen
over the last few years. Fieldfare, twite, tawny owl, barn owl,
ruff, curlew, heron, mallard, barnacle geese, peregrine falcon,
kestrel, buzzard, redshank, skylark, starling, wagtails,
magpie, wheatear, lapwings by the hundred which defend their
nests so fiercely, a little owl on a telegraph pole, a covey of
partridge on the road, snipe drumming in the evening air,
grouse calling 'go back, go back' from the heather of the moor,
a cuckoo shouting over the hill and a hen harrier being mobbed
by diving swallows, like a squadron of spitfires.

* One day on the road over the moor I divided a covey of
young grouse, the mother and four chicks going to one side of
the car and the rest to the other side. I got out to see if I
could see them, well aware of their ability at camouflage and
their equal ability to remain absolutely still. I stood on the
road verge not daring to move lest I trod on one of the young.
At first I could see nothing, and then, within inches of my
foot, I saw a bright eye fixed steadfastly on me. One by one I

picked out four young grouse, and the mother, within a yard of me and all as still as death. I got back into the car to allow the family to be re-united.

* We have little skill in botany but were recently visited by someone who has that skill. He came back from a walk excited by the many spring flowers, including orchids, which he had found.

* Today the shepherd brought the ewes and the fully grown lambs down to the farm. Here the lambs were separated from their mothers and put into a field near us. It will be a noisy night and sleep will be difficult, but in forty-eight hours they will have stopped bleating and forgotten their mothers.

* The summer is moving on and the swallows have been congregating on the power lines. Our roof faces south and the late sun warms it. Dozens of young swallows have gathered on it twittering and fluttering. Soon they will follow their parents to South Africa for the winter. By what instinct do they know the way?

* Late summer and autumn bring their special interests. Often there is a steam train on the Settle/Carlisle line and we can hear it whistle, echoing in our dale. One day a pack of foot hounds came down the dale following the walking huntsman. With the hounds were several young russell terriers yoked in pairs to stop them disappearing down every rabbit hole and having to be dug out. The hay had been late getting and the baler was traversing the valley. The terriers were into everything, and under every bale, noses sniffing.

* Tonight in the pitch dark I heard a piercing scream. There was no help for it, a rabbit had been caught by a stoat.

* Tonight the darkness of the dale was penetrated by narrow, intensly bright, shafts of light. They come from searchlights placed on the top of cars in which young farmers were looking for foxes which had robbed a hen roost. When the light picks out a fox he tends to stand still, mesmerised by it. That is a chance to shoot him with a .22 rifle.

* All day hikers have passed within a hundred yards of the house following the footpath up the dale past East House and Scale and making for Swarth Fell, Wild Boar Fell and Uldale. Every day in the summer we see them. One night in winter, in pouring rain, a woman soldier on a 24 hour survival exercise called asking for food, fearing all the time that she might be seen by a 'spotter' and disqualified. We had a few moment's chat in the porch without the light on and she left to find a place to sleep on the sodden ground.

* Today I saw a deer running alongside the fence of the recently planted conifer woods. Perhaps venison pasty is on its way back. Christmas is near. I must get some yule logs for the fire.

So the story might continue, as it has done for centuries. People come and go. Early man, Romans, Saxons, Vikings, Monks, Quakers, Methodists ... and who knows who will follow us? At some time the rabbit and the brown rat made their way into the dale. Three hundred years ago the last wild boar in England was killed on Wild Boar Fell, and the last wolf was hunted down somewhere on these northern hills. Birds, like the barn owl which feel the pressure of our modern society, find the dale a quiet haven. So do human beings under pressure who seek for a time to withdraw into places like Grisdale from the busy world outside.

Through all this the silent stream glides by, flowing on gently like Time which 'bears all its sons away'.

Yellow
Flag

YELLOW FLAG

118